Teach Them To Be Happy

by

Robert A. Sullo

New View Publications
Chapel Hill

This book is for Laurie, Kristy, Greg, and Melanie

Illustrations by Laurie A. Sullo

Cover design by Pamela Grimball

Library of Congress Cataloging-in-Publication Data
Sullo, Robert A., 1951-
        Teach Them To Be Happy
        1. Happiness in children. 2. Child rearing
I. Title
BF723.H37S85 1989   649.123   89-61056
ISBN 0-944337-17-1

Manufactured in the United States of America.

Acknowledgments

Dr. William Glasser's speaking and writing about Reality Therapy and Control Theory have helped me become a better parent and a happier, more effective person. I want to express my sincere appreciation to Dr. Glasser for sharing his vision in an articulate, concise, and helpful way.

The following people have been especially helpful to me in my growing understanding of Control Theory and Reality Therapy: Nancy Buck, Dave Hardy, Al Katz, and David Moran. Thank you all for adding quality to my life.

I have had the opportunity to train with many gifted instructors in the Institute of Reality Therapy. Each of them has shared wisdom unselfishly and I am especially grateful to Shelley Brierly, Jeanette McDaniel, Jeff Mintz, Bill Abbott, Bob Hoglund, and Fitz-George Peters.

Valuable input was provided by:
Sandy Boucher, Director, Sandy's School, Wareham, MA
Flo Szabo, Early Child Specialist, Plymouth Public
    Schools, Plymouth, MA
Shirley Keifer, Dallas Center-Grimes Kindergarten, Iowa
Valerie Fairhurst, Antioch Corporation, Cataumet, MA
Lynn Ingram, Plymouth-Carver Regional School System,
    Plymouth, MA
Christine Hmura, F.J. McGrath Elementary School,
    Worcester, MA
Delores Haberman, Principal, Bishop Pocock Catholic
    School, Saskatoon, Saskatchewan, Canada

This project was made much easier because of the support, encouragement, and enthusiasm of Perry and Fred Good. Thanks for believing in the value of this book. Thanks also to Nancy Salmon, editor of the first edition of this book, and to Angela Whitlock-Dove, who edited this revised edition with sensitivity, patience, and in the spirit of collaboration. Their efforts helped to make this a better, more readable book.

I'm fortunate to have parents who have given me the love, encouragement, and support every child should receive. Thank you for teaching me to be happy.

Finally, Laurie, Kristy, Greg, and Melanie remain my greatest teachers and help more than they realize. I am thankful that I have such a need-satisfying family.

Foreword

Happy children become good students and develop into responsible, independent adults. Bob Sullo shows parents and teachers how to teach Control Theory to very young people in a way that is fun and useful to them in their daily lives.

It is never too early to learn how people are motivated and why they behave as they do. Responsibly meeting our basic needs is critical to develop a positive self-concept and good, strong relationships in life. Children can acquire the skills which will help them know what they want and get what they need.

Teach Them To Be Happy has proven to be a significant contribution to the field of Reality Therapy and Control Theory. It has been successfully used by a growing number of teachers who are interested in the ideas I have presented in *The Quality School*. The revised, updated edition of *Teach Them To Be Happy* will provide even more activities for parents and teachers to use with young children as they begin their journey to quality.

William Glasser, M.D.
Los Angeles, California
April 1993

Preface

Knowing how to be happy is not as mysterious as it appears to be. Quality schools and families can only occur if each person involved, no matter how young, knows how to meet their needs effectively.

Bob Sullo has written a companion book based on my book, *In Pursuit of Happiness*, with examples and activities applicable to young children. *Teach Them To Be Happy* gives teachers and parents of young children a guide for systematically teaching children what they need and what they can do to be happy.

I hope that using these ideas with your own children or those you teach will be as exciting, gratifying, and fun for you as it has been for us.

Perry Good
Chapel Hill, NC
May 1993

Introduction To The Second Edition

One of the key components in the Reality Therapy process is to help people evaluate their own behavior. I began to evaluate *Teach Them To Be Happy* almost as soon as it was published. Though I was pleased, I knew that it would be a stronger, more valuable resource for both teachers and parents if it contained more activities. The revised edition of *Teach Them To Be Happy* contains many more activities than the original. In most cases, these activities have been suggested to me by practitioners who have found them particularly successful.

One of the most exciting aspects of practicing Reality Therapy is that ideas continue to evolve. This revised edition of *Teach Them To be Happy* has been written to include and expand on Dr. William Glasser's Quality School and Quality World concepts, applying them to the development of young children.

Writing, like all of life, is a process. This revised edition represents my growth as a writer and practitioner of Reality Therapy. I hope you will find wisdom and value in the following pages.

Bob Sullo
January 1993

Table of Contents

"It is not easy to find happiness in ourselves
and it is not possible to find it elsewhere."

Anges Repplier
The Treasure Chest

PART I

Using Control Theory
& Reality Therapy With
Young Children

Many young children, and even adults, believe that happiness is something that just "happens" to them, and that it is somehow unrelated to what they are doing. On the contrary, happiness is experienced when we satisfy our needs in a responsible way. Even young children can learn how to behave responsibly and gain more effective control of their lives once they make the connection between how they choose to behave and the level of happiness they experience.

I have written this book for professional educators, parents, and other adults who care deeply about and spend time with children three years old through third grade. This is a book about teaching young children to enjoy greater happiness. After reading and using this book, you will find that the children you deal with will begin to act more responsibly, understand the basic needs which motivate them, and see that they are in control of their behaviors and the happiness they will experience for the rest of their lives.

The ideas in this book are based largely on Dr. William Glasser's work in Reality Therapy and Control Theory. More specifically, this book builds upon E. Perry Good's *In Pursuit of Happiness*. A lively, animated, and exciting book, *In Pursuit of Happiness* has become a favorite of mine. My goal with *Teach Them To Be Happy* has been to write a book for parents and early childhood educators that is as valuable to use with children as *In Pursuit of Happiness* is with teens and adults.

As an educator for close to 20 years and a parent of three children, I feel strongly about the ideas presented on the following pages. The most telling comment I can make is that I use these ideas in my own life, with my own children, and I am a happier person and a better parent as a result. I sincerely hope that I can find the words to make these concepts come alive for you as well. If I am successful, your lives and the lives of the children you touch will be happier—and that's what this book is all about!

Teaching Control Theory and Reality Therapy concepts to young children fosters their cognitive development and leads to greater happiness for both you and them. Part I of this book provides a general overview so that you will have a frame of reference. In Part II, I will explain various aspects of Control Theory in more detail.

Control Theory and Reality Therapy

Control Theory contends that all of our behavior is internally motivated. We are all born with certain needs, both physical and psychological, which must be satisfied. Our behavior represents our best attempt at any given moment to meet our needs. Whenever we do something that helps us get more of what we need in a responsible way, it adds quality to our lives. These experiences are stored in a part of our memories called the Quality World, a collection of need-satisfying pictures which represents how we would like our lives to be. Although most people recognize their survival needs (food, sleep, warmth, etc.), they may not realize they have *psychological* needs which also must be satisfied. The four basic psychological needs are: love or belonging, power or competence, freedom, and fun. While not all behavior is effective or responsible, it is always the individual's attempt to satisfy one or more basic needs. Some "crazy" behavior is actually chosen by people because they believe that it offers them the best chance to meet their psychological needs. Control Theory teaches us that when people have more effective, responsible behaviors available to them to satisfy their needs, they will give up the less effective behaviors. Our role as parents and teachers is to help children develop effective behaviors and make responsible choices as they try to satisfy their needs.

Reality Therapy is the application of the principles of Control Theory. It is a process which includes asking people to examine what they want, what behaviors they are currently using to get what they want, and evaluating the effectiveness of these behaviors. Once a person realizes that their current behaviors are not the most effective, responsible behaviors available, they can choose more effective behaviors and make better decisions.

It is often difficult to get people to give up their current behavioral choices, even ineffective ones. It takes a lot of hard work, commitment, and faith for people to risk new behaviors. Young children have not had much time to develop ineffective behavior patterns. If they are given good instruction and a supportive environment, they will quickly learn to make more responsible choices. Even very young children can learn the basics of Control Theory and start to understand that their happiness is directly related to what they choose to do. Equipped with that powerful knowledge, they are less likely to blame others when things go wrong. They are less likely to wait passively for things to improve. They will learn to take effective action, choosing responsible behaviors that lead to happiness.

Control Theory is very different from stimulus-response theory, currently the most widely practiced and advocated psychological approach in America. stimulus-response theory asserts that when we reward behaviors they will increase in frequency. Similarly, we use punish-

4

ment to decrease the frequency of "negative" behaviors. Essentially, stimulus-response theory contends that we are controlled by outside forces, shaped by the presentation of rewards and punishments. Most educators have had some training in stimulus-response theory and many practice this approach routinely. Parents, too, are often attracted by this apparently "common-sense" explanation of what motivates their children's behavior.

Control Theory teaches that we are internally, not externally motivated. Whereas stimulus-response theory suggests that we are reactive creatures, looking to gain rewards from others or avoid their punishment, Control Theory states that we choose our behavior because we believe it will help us satisfy our basic needs.

Children who have been raised with a stimulus-response approach to child rearing, and educated in the same way frequently become rebellious and defiant. Following a stimulus-response model, many parents and educators resort to stronger punishments only to meet increased resistance. When we punish adolescents, we frustrate them and they often choose to disobey, in part to satisfy their needs for power and freedom. Children in preschool and the primary grades also choose their actions, but because they frequently choose what we want them to do, we mistakenly believe that we control them. In reality, young children often behave the way we want them to because at their age they rely heavily upon us to help them satisfy their needs. Experience shows us that people do what they believe is most need-fulfilling, not necessarily what we want them to do.

You may find yourself asking, "If punishment is ineffective and children are going to do what they want anyway, should we accept irresponsible, disruptive behavior?" Absolutely not! Discipline is both effective and essential. Unlike punishment, discipline works because it involves natural consequences (all behaviors have consequences) and it teaches responsibility.

"In nature there are neither
rewards nor punishments — there
are consequences."

Roger E. Ingersoll

An example may help clarify the difference between punishment and discipline and their respective effectiveness. "Time-out" is a *punishment* strategy frequently used with young children in which the misbehaving child is cut off from all activities and reinforcers. Once the "sentence" has been served, the child is allowed to rejoin the group, perhaps no wiser, a bit more angry, with his self-esteem compromised.

A frequently used Control Theory alternative to time-out is a planning center. Here, the misbehaving child (who has had numerous legitimate chances to behave more responsibly but continues to be disruptive) is removed from the group but is not punished in any way. In the planning center, the misbehaving child must come up with a plan for acceptable behavior in order to rejoin the group. Of course, most young children will need help developing a plan. In the planning center, an involved, caring adult helps children learn more responsible ways to satisfy their needs. There is no attempt to punish or to show the child "who is boss"—strategies which promote further irresponsibility and can damage a child's emerging self-concept. There is only a genuine attempt to help children become competent, effective, and responsible.

My younger daughter was two years old when my wife and I decided that we wanted to teach her responsibility rather than punish her. If our attempts to have Melanie give up unacceptable behaviors weren't successful, she would be told to go to her room until she could devise a plan to behave more responsibly. She was allowed to have fun, to be happy, and to retain power and self-esteem by determining when she was going to plan behaviors that would lead to her being allowed to join the rest of the family. Generally, she would play in her room for awhile, until she decided it would be more satisfying to join the rest of us downstairs. It was then that she would appear at the top of the stairs and announce, "I have a plan." When questioned what her plan was, she would almost always say, "I'm coming down now!" To expect much more of a two-year-old would have been foolish, so Melanie would come downstairs and we would help her develop more specific plans.

Effective discipline is not easy. It is easier to yell at or spank a misbehaving child than it is to take the time to help him develop a plan for more appropriate behavior. Punishment is especially attractive when children *seem* to behave much better when it is used. The hectic, stressful environment of a classroom populated by young children can make the short-term relief provided by punishment very alluring. Parents home with young children all day or those returning home after a hard day at work may find punishment an attractive quick-fix. But before you embrace the use of punishment, ask yourself these important questions: Are there long-term negative consequences to my use of punishment? Will punishment help this child? Will it help me get what I want in the long run? Can I choose a more effective behavior to help the child grow— to make better decisions and become more responsible? One that will help me become more like the ideal teacher or parent I would like to be? My guess is that once you answer these questions, punishment will never again be as attractive to you as it has been, and you will instead become an advocate for the use of firm discipline in your attempt to help children grow up responsibly.

Control Theory teaches us that we always have some control over what we do. Our lives, good or bad, happy or miserable, are largely the product of our choices. Control Theory stresses the concepts of freedom and responsibility. An unfortunate and unintentional by-product of a belief in stimulus-response theory is an abdication of personal responsibility. If I am taught that my actions are controlled by my parents' and teachers' use of punishments and rewards, I come to believe that my current life difficulties are not my fault. (e.g., "Everything would be fine if people would only pay more attention to what I'm saying." "The teachers in this school just don't know how to teach." "Gregory made me do it.") Blaming, getting angry, or feeling guilty or depressed may work for a while, but none of these strategies helps to solve difficulties in the long run. To live a more effective life and to be a happier person, you will have to act differently from how you are acting right now. That is a hard lesson to learn and one many of us hide from because it involves work, but it is also a powerful, exciting discovery. Along with the work comes the realization that you hold the key to your future happiness. You no longer have to look outside of yourself to find the road to a happier life. Just as you must confront the fact that you are choosing whatever pain you are presently experiencing, you can rejoice in the knowledge that you can make better choices beginning right now. You can choose happiness.

Developmental Appropriateness

Control Theory and Reality Therapy are used successfully with people of all ages, in any stage of development. However, the age and developmental level of your children has to be taken into consideration if you are to be effective in your use and teaching of Control Theory and Reality Therapy. The ideas and concepts presented in this book can be used successfully with children as young as two years old, but only if the child's developmental level is taken into consideration and the process applied accordingly. It is appropriate for you to ask two-year-old children to think, to see the connections among their behavioral choices, what happens to them, and their happiness. But expecting two-year-olds to plan more effective behaviors independently is folly. Asking young children to assume more responsibility than is developmentally possible will only lead to frustration. Using these concepts within a developmentally appropriate context will help children learn to meet their needs in a more responsible fashion.

It is not my purpose to discuss developmental issues in detail. Most early childhood educators have had courses in child development and are experienced in working with children. They understand how children typically behave at certain ages and during different stages of development. And many parents, even without formal training, have a good sense of what their child needs and what demands can be reasonably placed on their child. If you would like more information in this area, see the "Suggestions for Further Reading" section at the end of this book. The most important thing for you to remember is that children have special needs because of their age, their level of development, and their individuality. Keep this in mind as you implement the ideas presented in this book.

A Special Note To Classroom Teachers

A major focus in the Quality School movement concerns the distinction between "teaching" and "managing." Whereas teaching involves imparting skills and information to people who want to learn, managing requires us to help people discover that what we are asking them to do will add quality to their lives. Many of our colleagues who work with older children enter education expecting to "teach," only to find that they spend more time "managing." Those of us who have the chance to work with young children are fortunate because most young children come to us already believing that we have something valuable to offer them, that being successful in our programs will, indeed, add quality to their lives. Consequently, we operate in an environment where teaching and learning in their purest forms can flourish.

To promote optimum growth, teachers want to create an environment which encourages children to satisfy their four basic psychological needs: love, power, fun, and freedom. Remember that our behavior is an attempt to satisfy these needs. An environment in which these needs are consistently met fosters healthy development. Discipline problems decrease in a setting where children's needs are met within child-initiated, teacher-sanctioned activities. There is less cause for children to engage in inappropriate, disruptive behavior to meet their needs.

Think for a minute about some of the misbehavior you deal with daily. Is it possible that the disruptive child is choosing that behavior in an attempt to meet his need for personal power? If so, remember that the child's need for power can't be turned off. If you were able to develop activities which would allow him to meet his need for power appropriately, his disruptive behavior would diminish significantly and you would both be a lot happier.

Take some time to think about the activities you currently use with your children and ask yourself this question: What need or needs are addressed by this activity? I'm willing to guess that every activity satisfies one or more of the four basic psychological needs. I also believe that some activities satisfy more needs than others, and these are probably your most popular, successful activities. One key to building a successful educational program is making sure that the activities chosen by adults and children are diverse enough to address each of the four basic psychological needs on a daily basis. Optimum growth and development can occur only in an environment where all four basic needs are met in a balanced way. If you offer a choice of activities with this premise in mind, you will be on your way to creating a more effective educational program.

Using This Book

Each chapter in *Teach Them To Be Happy* is divided into two sections: "Think It" and "Do It." "Think It" introduces a Control Theory concept and explains how it is relevant to the lives of young children. "Do It" consists of age-appropriate activities for children so they can practice Control Theory and learn how to choose happiness.

The initial activity for most chapters allows you to introduce the highlighted concept using a puppet. Children love puppets, and teachers are well aware of their educational value. Parents can use puppets with children at home just as easily. As you introduce various Control Theory concepts, your children will remain interested and learn more because puppets help make learning fun.

For each of these intro-ductory activities, I have provided a sample dialogue between you and "Do-It," a flying snail puppet. Pat-terned after Jeff Hale's illustrations in Perry Good's book *In Pursuit of Happiness*, "Do-It" the flying snail is an appealing, fanciful creature. With its cheerful colors, friendly  expression, and golden wings, it symbolizes love, power, fun and freedom—the essential concepts of happiness. ("Do-It" puppets can be ordered from New View Publica-tions, P. O. Box 3021, Chapel Hill, NC 27515.) If you do not have a "Do-It" puppet, use any other appealing puppet you have, or fashion a simple puppet from an old sock by drawing features with colorful fabric markers, perhaps adding a couple of buttons for eyes. I cannot overemphasize that the dialogues are simply to guide you, to get you going, especially if you have not had many opportunities to use puppets in the past. Once you become comfortable with puppet dialogues, I am confident you will be developing your own.

The puppet activities are usually followed by "Happy Book" activities. Children, with adult help if needed, complete pages in the companion activity book *I'm Learning To Be Happy* (also available from New View Publications). This experience helps the children solidify their understanding of each concept. Additional activities are included in each of the chapters.

All of the activities included in Part II have been designed for children three years old through the third grade. I have attempted to suggest activities which can be used both at home and in school, individually and in groups, by children at various stages of development. Some activities may be used more readily in given settings or with children of a particular age, but most of the activities can be easily adapted for your particular situation.

A number of whole language advocates have found that *I'm Learning To Be Happy* can be used successfully and comfortably within their classrooms. In a whole language classroom, students are immersed in an environment rich in reading, writing, and oral communication. Many teachers create "big book" versions of *I'm Learning to be Happy*. These large, colorful adaptations based upon student work are read and enjoyed by the entire class. The result is a highly readable book that the children have "written," allowing them to have a sense of authorship and ownership—important components within the whole language philosophy. Groups of young learners in these classrooms are being introduced to reading and writing in an enjoyable and developmentally appropriate way. The whole language philosophy is an important one in education and consistent with the concepts being introduced in *Teach Them To Be Happy*.

There is not one "right" way to use this book; a number of approaches are equally valid. I suggest that you read through the entire text before you begin to implement any of the ideas or activities with your children to be sure that you are fully acquainted with Control Theory. After a first reading, you will have to forge your own path. Some preschool teachers have successfully based a one- or two-month unit of study on the ideas and activities presented here. The Control Theory orientation is then woven into a pre-existing program. Others may find that the material works into their current programs more comfortably if they use the activities once a week or one week a month. A number of elementary school counselors have developed 8-15 session groups using *I'm Learning To Be Happy* to teach Control Theory to children in the early grades. Parents, too, may find particular approaches work better with their children. Experiment to see which approach best fits your situation.

For those of you who want more direction from the author, I will share my personal bias. I favor a "focused" approach as a first step for educators or parents. I suggest moving right through the book, using the activities in a systematic way to give the children an overall sense of what choosing happiness is all about. Then return to specific concepts and activities on a regular basis to review what the children have learned. This second phase represents an on-going Control Theory approach to teaching and parenting which I believe helps children grow up to be happier and more responsible. However, this is only one "right" way. I am delighted to hear from readers who share other successful approaches they have implemented.

Before you begin Part II, I invite you to pause for a moment and consider what you are about to begin. You are about to help children learn specific ways to meet their needs more responsibly in an increasingly complex world. You are about to help children learn that they are largely in control of their own lives and their own happiness— that they are not controlled from the outside, but from within. You are providing your children with a gift that some people may never receive, and others receive only in adulthood: the knowledge that they can choose to lead happier, more productive lives regardless of their current circumstances. That is a precious gift, one which every child deserves.

Ralph Waldo Emerson, wrote in *Nature*, "Good thoughts are no better than good dreams, unless they be executed!" Translated into Control Theory terms: After you think it, DO IT!

Chapter One: Our Basic Needs

Too many of us think of happiness as a product, as something we can "achieve," like more money or more material possessions. In reality, happiness is a process by which we satisfy our basic psychological needs in a balanced, varied way. Just as importantly, we can't simply decide to *feel* happier. In order to *be* happier and more successful in our lives, we have to think and act. When children feel sad, successful teachers and parents encourage them to do something different (to join the group, to play a game, etc.) The sadness is usually replaced by happiness, the result of doing something more effective and need-satisfying. Still, many people continue to see *feeling* as separate from doing and thinking, but it's not.

Helping children make this connection is one of the major goals of this book.

Let's look at each of the basic psychological needs in detail to develop an understanding of what they are:

 LOVE can be seen as belonging, friendship, and caring about others. Consider all the people in your life and determine the people with whom you have a deep, caring relationship. Most of us have several people who fall into this category, but every one of us needs at least one person to whom we feel especially close. The same is true for children. Thankfully, most children are loved by parents, grandparents, brothers, and sisters. Teachers can love their students, and most children feel a special fondness for their first teachers. For less fortunate children who may be victims of abuse, neglect, or abandonment, the need to love and be loved may be difficult to satisfy because they lack the social skills and behaviors which would make them attractive to others. A vicious cycle of failure is initiated. Unloved children seek love in increasingly ineffective and desperate ways, only to find themselves further mired in social isolation. Their need for love, however, is just as strong. Our goal is to help all of the children in our lives meet their need for love, whether that be in our schools or our homes.

 POWER is perhaps the most misunderstood of the basic needs because we tend to think of it exclusively as power over other people. In reality, the need for power refers to personal power, a sense of competence, and a sense of doing things well. It includes recognition that what you do and who you are is important. An important form of recognition involves self-evaluation. You can remind yourself daily that you are competent, that you have certain specific talents, and that you are important. Far from being self-centered and egotistical, self-appreciation based upon honest self-evaluation helps satisfy the need for power. Children can be recognized daily for the things they do well. Most teachers routinely provide children with recognition for appropriate behavior. Comments like the following help children meet their need for power: "That's a wonderful drawing, Jonathan!", "I like the way you and Sarah cooperated, Beth.", "Good talking, Kevin. I like it when you use your words." Also, children can participate regularly in short activities which recognize classmates for skills they have displayed and identify skills and competencies within themselves. Similar activities can be done at home. Frequently at dinner, my wife and I will ask our three children to identify two things they did well that day. Engaging in honest self-evaluation of our behaviors is a key component in building healthy self-esteem. We want our children to see that they demonstrate competence every day, not just on those special days when they have finally mastered a prized skill. This also helps children learn that the most important aspect of satisfying our needs is the *process*, not the product.

 FUN is a basic psychological need as important as any other. It involves laughter, joy, and the discovery of learning. Most children are adept at having fun. They play as often as they can and learn more before they begin their formal education than they will ever learn again in a comparable age

span. Generally adults are less skillful at having fun and some even go so far as to see fun in negative terms ("childish behavior"). It is important to recognize that there is an intimate connection between fun and learning. Watch children at play. They are constantly discovering, learning, and having fun. Whenever any of us, old or young, discovers something new, there is a sense of wonder, excitement, and fun that accompanies the learning. One of the saddest, most ironic comments a teacher can make is, "We're not here to have fun; we're here to learn." Having fun and learning are not at odds; they are mutually supportive. Parents who wish to raise happy, inquisitive children should provide them with as many fun activities as possible. When your children are having fun, they are simultaneously learning and satisfying their basic psychological needs.

 FREEDOM involves the ability to make choices. We are fortunate to live in a society that gives us considerable freedom, and most of us make countless choices every day. Even those who have never heard of Control Theory talk about the importance of giving children choices. Two points are especially important to keep in mind. The first is that you need to help children realize that they do make many choices every day. At home, many of them choose what clothes to wear. Preschool programs often have times in the day when children select from a variety of approved activities. Some elementary schools incorporate "free time" into their day, a time when children are given freedom, provided they engage in a worthwhile educational activity. Children will be happier if they understand that their need for freedom is regularly satisfied, making it easier for them to

cooperate when requested. There are times when children will be asked to remain quiet, put toys away, clean an area of the room, or listen to a teacher or parent. These limitations are accepted easily by children who are aware that they make many choices every day. The second point that merits emphasis is that we often restrict ourselves, making it very difficult to satisfy the need for freedom. You may know some children who fall into this category, unwilling or unable to let themselves go, to experience life fully. In a very real way, these children are victims of self-imprisonment. As long as they limit themselves, they will frustrate their need for freedom and be unable to experience all of the happiness they otherwise could. You will be helping these children immensely if you can find a way to let them take some risks and successfully meet their need for freedom.

To be truly happy we need to satisfy each of our four basic psychological needs regularly, responsibly, and in a balanced way. Sounds simple, right? It's not. If it were, we'd live in a far happier world. Take a look around you and find a child who doesn't seem to be particularly happy. As you consider his unhappiness, you will probably realize that he is having a hard time satisfying one or more of his basic needs in a responsible way. Until he finds and uses more effective behaviors to meet his needs, the unhappiness will persist. Conversely, once he begins to use more effective behaviors, he will immediately begin to feel happier. It can't be overstated: feelings are directly related to what a person chooses to do. If someone wants to feel happier, they will have to *do* something different from what they currently are doing.

Even though we all share the basic psychological needs of love, power, fun, and freedom, there are many different behaviors we can choose to satisfy these needs. If Megan has well-developed fine motor skills, she may find cutting and pasting activities satisfying, helping her to meet her needs for fun and power. If Jordan's fine motor skills are less developed, these same activities may be torturous for him. Still, he is driven to satisfy the same needs, so he has to search for other behaviors that will work for him. If he has well-developed gross motor skills and has a chance to play on the jungle gym, he will probably be able to meet his needs for fun and power in that way. If he does not have the opportunity to satisfy his needs responsibly, he may create disruptive behaviors in his attempt to gain power and recognition. The behaviors we choose to fulfill our needs reflect our individuality. It is important that each of us discover effective behaviors that work for us and accept the same in others. The only "rule" is that the behaviors we choose should allow us to satisfy our needs without interfering with another's attempt to satisfy his or her needs. Only you can know what makes you happy, and only I can know what makes me happy. We each need to find out what works for us individually and then do it!

Establishing the Environment

Before beginning any activities, either at home or at school, it is wise to establish an environment with the children. In fact, it may be beneficial to begin each activity with a quick review of behavioral expectations. The few minutes it takes can set a positive tone and discourage inappropriate behaviors that can detract from the experience.

While you will need to develop guidelines which meet your specific circumstances, the following can be used almost anywhere:

1. Children are expected to accept the choices and comments of the others in the group.

2. The group will not tolerate any negative feedback. If children believe that their comments will be criticized, they will quickly learn that silence is the best policy and your group will not be successful.

3. Adults will have to be careful not to "edit" what children say. If the children offer inappropriate suggestions, take the opportunity to explore the consequences of their suggestion.

Activity #1: The Need for Love

Your first activity will introduce children to "Do-It" the flying snail (or any other puppet character you choose) who will help them to learn how to live happier lives. In the initial activity, Do-It discusses the need for love and belonging.

What follows is a sample script. Feel free to modify it to suit your needs, style of speaking, and the developmental level of the child or children you are working with. The dialogue has been written for group use, but it can be easily modified for a single child.

You: I have a friend I want you to meet today. My friend is named "Do-It," and Do-It has some interesting things to tell us.

Do-It: Thanks. Hi, kids! It's great fun for me to get to visit with you. I don't know if I've ever seen such a happy group of kids before.

Y: Well, Do-It, that's one of the things we like about it here. We try to help everyone be happy.

D: And that's just what I wanted to talk about with all of you: some of the things that we need to help us be happy.

Y: What do you mean, Do-It?

D: We all need certain things to make us happy. One of them is love. Everybody in the whole world needs somebody they really love and care about, and who loves them, too. I bet the children have some people in their lives that they love. Can we ask them?

Y: Sure. (To the children) Can any of you tell Do-It the name of someone you really love who loves you, too?

At this point Do-It and the children can discuss various people who help the children meet their need for love and belonging, why these people are special, and how these people add quality to their lives. While Do-It and the children create a master list, you can put all of the class contributions on a large piece of newsprint or poster board. This master list should be displayed proudly in the room with the heading "People We Love." Parents completing this activity at home with their children can create a list to put on the wall or refrigerator. (While it is hardly the objective of this book, these activities are helpful pre-reading experiences for preschool children and will strengthen the reading skills of elementary school children.) Once the list has been completed, finish your dialogue with Do-It.

Y: Well, thanks, Do-It. I think we all had a good time and learned that love makes us happy.

D: There's more to it than that. If you'd like, I'd be glad to come back and talk about the other things we need in order to be happy.

Y: That would be wonderful, Do-It. Why don't we plan to have you talk with us again soon. (Note: If

possible, set a specific day and time when Do-It
will talk with the children again.)

D: That sounds good to me. Thanks, kids! I'll look
forward to talking to you again.

Activity #2: The Need for Power

In this dialogue, Do-It introduces the need for power.
With young children, I tend not to use the word "power."
Instead, ask the children to tell Do-It things they can do
well, what they are proud of doing, or times when they
feel important. Nearly all children are proud of something
they do. It doesn't matter what children say as long as it
represents something that makes them feel powerful or
competent.

You: Good morning, Do-It. It's nice to see you again.

Do-It: Hi, everybody. I hope all of you are happy this
morning. Remember the other day we talked about
how important it is to have people to love? Today, I
want to talk about another thing we all need to be
happy. I need your help again to make another list.
O.K.?

Y: What should I do, Do-It?

D: You can help by writing down what we say, just
like the last time. Hey, there's your other list! You
left it up on the wall. That's great! Look at all those
"People We Love."

Y: What's a good name for this list, Do-It?

26

D: Let's call this one "Things We Do Well." I bet everybody here does something very well. To be happy, we need to know that we can be successful, that there are things we do well. It makes us feel good to know we're good at some things, even if we can't do everything. Can any of you tell me something you do well, something you're proud of doing?

Follow the procedure you used in the activity for love, accepting all suggestions and creating a master list. Again, it's important for the children to have a chance to tell why these activities are meaningful for them. The process of sharing skills with classmates is as valuable as the list you will create. When finished, end your conversation with Do-It, making plans to have another conversation soon about the other things we need to make us happy.

Activity #3: The Need for Freedom
In this dialogue, Do-It introduces the need for freedom to the children. Children may have some difficulty understanding the concept of freedom, so Do-It will talk to them about choices. You could begin by listing some choices that we make at home or in school. As soon as someone mentions "I picked out this shirt," you'll quickly have a large list of choices children make and they'll see, perhaps for the first time, that they are given many options throughout the day. Even for children unable to read, there is something powerfully liberating about a wall hanging that announces "Choices We Make."

You: Hi, Do-It. We're glad to see you.

Do-It: And I'm glad to see all of you again. I hope that all of you have been doing things that make you happy.

Y: We've been trying our best. You said you had even more things you wanted to talk about with us.

D: That's right. Today I want to talk about choices.

Y: What do you mean "choices"?

D: Well, to be really happy, you have to have some freedom. You have to be able to make some choices.

Y: What kinds of choices?

D: Just choices. I bet you give the kids some choices here. (To the kids) Is that true? Who can tell me about some of the choices you have here? (To you) Will you write this down for us?

Y: Sure, Do-It. What do you want to call this list?

D: How about "Choices We Make"? O.K., kids, let's hear about some of the choices you make.

At the conclusion of this activity, make plans for Do-It to come back to discuss the remaining basic psychological need, fun.

Activity #4: The Need for Fun

In this activity, Do-It will talk with the children about the things they do for fun. The need for fun will probably be the easiest to discuss. Children are usually good at having fun and can identify what they do for fun. Perhaps the greatest problem you will face here will be children making critical comments about another child's selection. This is especially true with older children who are much more selective and judgmental about which activities are fun for them personally. You may want to stress with your group that all suggestions are "right" for the person who made them, that it's O.K. for them to disagree, but that they don't need to voice their disagreement. With most children, as long as their ideas are given recognition (power), they are willing to tolerate someone else's idea of fun. Once the list has been generated, your wall can be decorated with a poster that tells everyone "Things We Do For Fun."

You: Good morning, Do-It.

Do-It: Good morning. Hi, everybody. Boy, am I excited today.

Y: How come?

D: Today, I get to talk with you about one more thing we need in order to be happy. We have already talked about having people to love, of having things we can do well, and being able to make choices.

Y: What else is there?

D: One other thing everybody needs is fun! Does everybody here like to have fun? Hey, let's make another list. We can call it "Things We Do For Fun."

Y: O.K., Do-It. I have paper to make a list. (To the children) Remember, raise your hands and listen to everybody else so we can all enjoy this activity.

D: Let's begin. Who would like to tell me something they do that's fun?

Again, create a master list of activities, making sure that each child has an opportunity to contribute if they choose. As the children discuss what they like to do, they will be improving their speaking and listening skills.

Y: Well, Do-It, I want to thank you for coming and telling us about all the things we need in order to be happy.

D: It has been my pleasure. I like helping people learn about what they need to be happy. It makes it easier to be happy if you know what you need.

Y: I think I know what you mean. Well, Do-It, we're all going to miss you around here.

D: I could come back if you want. I still have lots more to share with you and the kids. And being with all of you is one of the things I do to make me happy. Would it be O.K. if I came back again sometime?

Y: Do-It, I think that would be wonderful. What do you think, children? It sounds like they'd like to see you, too, Do-It.

D: Great. I'll be here when you need me. Bye for now, kids!

Children at home or in school can decorate the posters they have made with drawings, photographs, or pictures cut from old magazines depicting how they meet their needs.

Activities # 5-8: Happy Book Activities

These four follow-up activities ("People I Love," "Things I Do Well," "Choices I Make," and "Things I Do For Fun") are designed for children to complete individually, with your help. The follow-up activities allow the children to reflect upon what they have discussed with Do-It. By completing these activities, children will solidify their understanding of the basic psychological needs.

Once the children generate master lists for each of the four basic needs, they are ready to make their own individual lists. The activity pages in *I'm Learning To Be Happy*, the companion activity-book, are designed for individual children to record their own answers for the activities offered here, creating a personal memory album as they are introduced to these concepts. Notice that for each activity, there are three spaces for each basic need. I have included only three lines so that children won't feel bad if they are unable to fill up an entire page. After completing the group activity with Do-It, each child should be able to list three people or activities for each basic need. Let them keep going, though, if they want to include more.

Most children are going to need adult assistance to complete their *I'm Learning To Be Happy* books. Many of them will be unable to read or write, so an adult will have to help them by reviewing the group list and letting them choose what they want to include in their individual books. It's critically important that children be allowed to choose what they want. We may think they should include family members on the "People I Love" page, whereas they may choose friends. Don't edit their choices. If they get the idea that there are "right" and "wrong" answers, they will quickly develop strategies to figure out what answers you want them to provide (to help them satisfy their need for love and belonging), and the activities will have far less real value and meaning.

Feel free to adapt all of the activities in this book to fit the needs of the children you serve. You may find the introductory activities with Do-It to be good energizers, while working on *I'm Learning To Be Happy* is better suited for quiet times and can be done later in the day. Try to end each activity with a discussion about the importance of what the children have done. Processing what has been done and encouraging the children to evaluate its worth are important aspects of introducing Control Theory to children. Let them know, in language they can understand, that these things are the keys to being happy and that together you are going to discover how to be happy as often as possible. While they may not be able to grasp everything you are telling them, you will be getting children to think—an important goal in itself. Just as importantly, you will get them to start thinking about ways to create more happy moments in their lives. That's a possibility that most of us, young or old, will gladly spend time considering.

A special note to school counselors: A number of elementary school counselors are using *I'm Learning To Be Happy* in counseling groups to help build self-esteem and increase responsibility. Some have shared with me that initially they had some concerns about the "directive" nature of the pages. To their surprise and my delight, they report that children find many creative ways to individualize and personalize their "Happy Books."

People I Love

_____

_____

_____

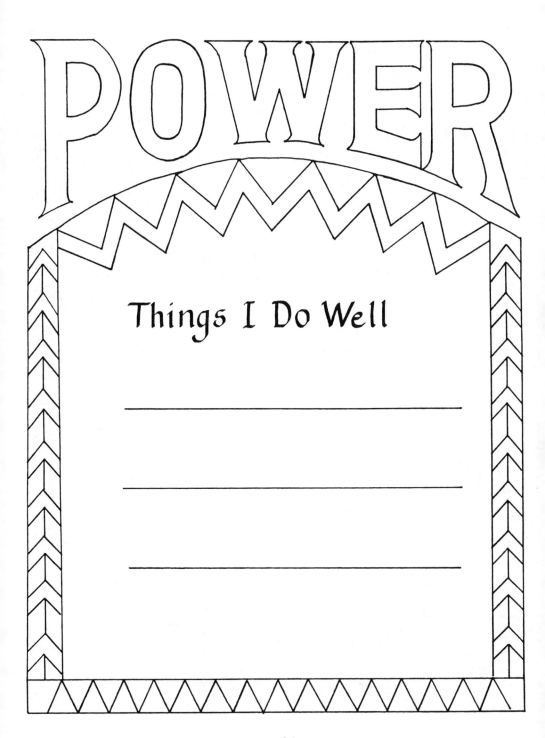

POWER

Things I Do Well

_____

_____

_____

35

Choices I Make

_____

_____

_____

FUN

Things I Do For Fun

_____

_____

_____

Additional Activities To Teach Basic Needs

Activity #9: Photo Album (Love)

Have the child tell you the names of some people or pets he or she loves. If this activity is done in a school setting and the child mentions some classmates, take pictures of those classmates. Gather together some photographs of people and pets the child has mentioned and glue the pictures onto paper, forming a book. Staple the pages together and on the front include the title "People I Love" and the child's name.

Activity #10: Pictures Of Success (Power)

At school or at home, take pictures of something a child has done particularly well and make a bulletin board labeled "Pictures of Success." (Example: Jodi standing next to a block building she has constructed.) Educators, be certain that every child has the opportunity for his or her "Picture of Success" to be on the bulletin board regularly.

Activity #11: The Power Of Media

A number of popular children's stories have been made into filmstrips or movies. Why not show one which will give children the chance to discuss the importance of power, success, and recognition? While there are many to choose from, *The Little Train That Could* is almost certain to be a success.

Activity #12: Puzzle Power

Many young children are skilled at putting together puzzles. Have an area in your home or class where a puzzle is left for the children to work on in their spare time. Every time a child adds another piece, he or she responsibly satisfies the need for power.

Activity # 13: What You Do Is Important

There are a variety of routine chores which need to be accomplished in all classrooms. Students can develop a legitimate sense of importance if they are involved in these tasks. Children can help with taking the attendance, changing the calendar, distributing the materials required to complete an activity, etc. The same concept applies at home. Even young children can help set the table, clean their rooms, and make their beds. All of these activities help children develop a healthy self-esteem as they begin to realize that what they do really matters.

Activity # 14: The Choice Is Yours

In the classroom, there are certain routines which occur according to a pre-set schedule. Still, there may be instances when there is a degree of flexibility in scheduling. At these times, why not let the children help you decide when particular activities will occur? Everything that needs to be addressed will be, and the children will probably be more cooperative and productive because you have created an environment in which they can meet their need for freedom.

Activity #15: Yes, We're Having Fun!

Fun is the payoff for learning. It is important for young children to realize as soon as possible that there is a strong connection between learning and having fun. As adults, we can help children make this connection both in school and at home. Whenever we observe children learning and having fun, we do them a favor by helping them appreciate the connection between the pleasure they are feeling and the learning they are doing.

Activity #16: We Have Fun In This Class!

In elementary schools, children traditionally have lots of opportunity for fun during non-academic times: physical education, art, music, etc. So much academic material needs to be addressed in the classroom that teachers can sometimes forget how important it is for students to have fun. One easy way to help remind yourself of the importance and value of fun is to post a sign in your room which announces to everyone: "We Have Fun In This Class!"

Activity # 17: Meeting My Needs In Class

One of our prime objectives as educators is to help children keep the picture of school in their Quality Worlds. Most children come to school eager to learn and believe that school will be a positive experience. Children who maintain this Quality World picture of school tend to be successful, driven by their need to establish competence and to achieve. The following activities take only a few minutes, but can serve as powerful affirmations of school as a need-satisfying part of the child's world.

"Cloze" activities provide students with sentences to complete. They can be structured for any of the basic needs, allowing children the chance to reflect about how school is need-satisfying. Here's an example of an activity based on the need for fun:

"I have fun in class when I _____, _____, and _____.

I have fun with _____ and _____."

Similar activities can be easily constructed for the other basic needs. These activities may be done individually by children. For example, they might be used by students who have completed an assignment before the rest of the class. Instead of having "free time," the students actively affirm why this class is need-satisfying, solidifying the position of school in their Quality Worlds.

Activity #18: Big Friends, Little Friends

This activity represents an ongoing strategy. In a school which services children of different ages, it is sometimes possible to pair the youngest with the oldest. These "Big Friend—Little Friend" relationships can help foster an atmosphere of cooperation and belonging in the school. The older children can help the younger with academic tasks or read stories to younger children. Additionally, the older children can meet their need for power by helping their "little friends." Sometimes the "Big Friend—Little Friend" groups can get together to play games. In schools where this has been done, teachers have noted a marked decrease in the teasing that occurs in school.

Activity #19: Reading Is Need-Satisfying

One of the most important and need-satisfying activities we can do with young children is to read to them or with them. Reading aloud to children is critically important for a number of reasons. First, on the most basic level, it means you and the child are spending quality time together. Second, there is ample research to indicate that children who are read to regularly develop into better readers and more successful students. Third, children will learn from experience that reading is a worthwhile leisure activity.

While there is almost no type of reading which will not strengthen your relationship and help your child grow, certain books can be particularly helpful if you want to discuss basic needs. If you read any of the following books with your children at home or in class, you will have an opportunity to more fully discuss the basic needs with them and help them to understand how these needs motivate us throughout our lives. Most of the books suggested are recommended by Jim Trelease in the *Read Aloud Handbook*. All books are written at a kindergarten through grade three reading level, so the children may be able to read to you, providing another opportunity for them to demonstrate competence and power. I have tried to arrange the books according to what specific basic need is addressed, but many books present opportunities to discuss a number of these needs.

Love and Belonging

The Giving Tree, Shel Silverstein
A Taste of Blackberries, Doris Buchanan Smith
The Mountain That Loved A Bird, Alice McLerran
The Pain & The Great One, Judy Blume

Grandaddy's Place, Helen V. Griffith
Rosalie, Joan Hewett
Always Gramma, Vaunda Micheaux Nelson
I'll Always Love You, Hans Wilhelm
Hey, Al, Arthur Yorinks & Richard Egielski
Happy Birthday, Grampie, Susan Pearson
I'll Love You Forever, Robert Muench
Brenda & Edward, Marian Kovalski

Power (Success)

The One In The Middle Is The Green Kangaroo,
   Judy Blume
Annebelle Swift, Kindergartner, Amy Schwartz
Rachel and Obadiah, Brinton Turkle
Swimmy, Leo Lionni
Brave Irene, William Steig
Sleep Out, Carol & Donald Carrick

Freedom (Decision-Making, Individuality)

William's Doll, Charlotte Zolotow
Awful Thursday, Ron Roy
Thy Friend Obadiah, Brinton Turkle
Oh, The Places You'll Go, Dr. Seuss
I Want A Dog, Dayal Kaur Khalsa

Fun

Ira Sleeps Over, Bernard Waber
Frederick, Leo Lionni
Two Bad Ants, Chris Van Allsburg
Miss Nelson Is Missing, Harry Allard
Best Friends for Francis, Russell Hoban
What Happened To Patrick's Dinosaurs?,
   Carol Carrick

Chapter Two: Signals

This chapter is about signals, those vital messages that let us know if we are meeting our needs. Every one of us knows, at every moment, just how we want the world to be at that particular time. We have a mental "picture" of what represents a high quality experience. At the same time, our senses and perceptions are monitoring what is going on in the real world. These two images are being constantly compared. If the real world seems to be like the Quality World picture I have in my head at that moment, I get a positive signal. If the world as I perceive it is different from my Quality World picture, I get a negative signal. Signals are vital. Without signals, we wouldn't know if we were meeting our needs, and without that knowledge we wouldn't know if we were happy or sad.

Signals last only an instant and are felt internally. We aren't even consciously aware of them. They are felt as an urge to behave, encouraging us to continue a behavior that leads to a positive signal or to change behaviors if we're getting a negative signal. The interval between receiving a signal and behaving is nearly imperceptible, especially in young children. Watch young children for a while and you'll soon be given a glimpse of their internal signals. When they are engaged in satisfying behaviors, their brains are pumping out positive signals and the children are driven to sustain those behaviors. That's why children, despite their limited attention span, will sometimes spend long periods of time engaging in an activity and become visibly upset when they are told that they must stop doing it. Negative signals work in the same way. When young children are not meeting their needs, they feel a negative signal and almost immediately act upon it, making us aware, through their behavior, that their needs are not satisfied. They will yell, hit, throw things, sulk, have a tantrum, switch activities, or engage in any other behavior they think has a reasonable chance of helping them more successfully meet their needs. Each of us has our own individual system of signals that let us know whether we are meeting our basic needs.

The more you become aware of your signals, both positive and negative, the more you will be able to effectively control how happy you are. As elementary as it sounds, one of the first steps in improving your level of happiness is to figure out just where you are now. Recognizing your signals will help you immensely.

Of course, not all signals are equally strong. A child momentarily unable to locate her mother experiences a negative signal that is jolting in its strength. There is a

massive discrepancy between the information coming in and the Quality World picture she has in her head. Once she locates her mother, walking towards her with open arms, an equally strong positive signal sweeps over her and bathes her in momentary, pure ecstasy. Most signals are far less extreme. Our days are characterized by minor triumphs and little annoyances, each producing signals, but most of us are less adept at identifying these important markers. In many ways these subtler signals are just as important as the louder signals because a major portion of our overall happiness is determined by routine, everyday events. Most young children can tell you why their birthday party was a success ("Everybody gave me presents!" "We got to eat cake *and* ice cream!" "All my friends were there!"), but it takes much more skill and effort to tell what made an ordinary day a success. It takes considerable practice to recognize and act effectively on the minor signals we get every waking hour of every day, but it is worth the effort because it enriches our lives.

It's ironic how quickly we attend to the signals tied to survival, while many of us ignore the signals tied to our psychological needs. When we get a "hunger" signal, we eat. When we get a "cold" signal, we put on a sweater. But too many of us try to ignore the signals related to our psychological needs, even when we recognize them. Why? For many, it is simply because we don't know what to do when we recognize "angry," "depressed," or "scared" signals. So we try to ignore them, hoping they'll just go away. The problem is that they do not go away. Signals are messengers and they won't stop until the message has been delivered. And as far as the signals are concerned, the message hasn't been delivered until we do something. The message is always the same: we don't have enough

love, power, fun, or freedom in our lives right now. To get rid of the negative signal, you'll have to do something different, something which helps you satisfy your needs more effectively.

Once you acknowledge a negative signal, take responsibility by doing something to get what you need. In a very real way, if you don't do something different, you are choosing the misery you will continue to experience. That's a difficult concept for many people to accept. They find it easier to blame their feelings, especially their miserable ones, on other people. ("You make me so angry!") But other people don't *make* us anything. We receive the negative signal that the world is not the way we want it to be right now, that our needs are not being satisfied, and we choose anger, depression, or guilt, because we hope it will satisfy our needs. If my son Gregory misbehaves, he doesn't *make* me angry. When I receive a negative signal, I may choose anger because I believe that showing anger will help me get what I want. It usually works, in the short run. Because of Greg's need for love and belonging, he will usually choose to behave in a way that I define as appropriate. All of us who deal with young children have to ask ourselves: (1) Are there long-term negative consequences to choosing anger regularly in order to get what we want? and (2) What other, more effective behaviors could we choose when we receive negative signals?

Many people blame their feelings and behaviors on others. Some don't want to do the hard work of getting what they want in a responsible way. Others believe that no matter what they do, they won't get what they want anyway. If you are in one of these categories, you'll have to give up these attitudes in order to live a happier life.

Becoming responsible for your own happiness may be tough, but it's necessary if you want to be happy.

Recognizing Positive Signals

Our brain has developed to help us survive. It is no surprise, therefore, that we are much better at recognizing negative signals than positive ones. While this may be advantageous for survival, it doesn't do much to help us become more happy. If we want to be happier, we have to do a better job of recognizing what we do to satisfy our needs.

One thing which distinguishes happy people from unhappy people is that happy people are more aware of what they are doing "right." This insight helps them savor life more completely and provides them with a blueprint for future behaviors. Children can become more aware of what they are doing when they receive positive signals and feel happy. We can assist by helping them make the connection between the behavior they are currently choosing and the good feeling they are experiencing. I frequently do this with my children. Their facial expressions tell me that they are receiving powerful positive signals at that moment. So that they won't make the common mistake of believing that happiness just "happened" to them, I ask them to identify what they are doing at that moment. I then ask them how they are feeling. Over time, they will make the connection between acting and feeling, and learn that they can voluntarily choose from a repertoire of

behaviors which will help them experience happiness on a regular basis.

Recognizing Negative Signals

We are skilled at recognizing negative signals, especially the loud ones. If we want to be happier, however, we'll have to become aware of and do something about the quieter negative signals we tend to ignore. Ignoring negative signals would make more sense if the signals just went away, but they don't. In fact, ignoring subtle signals often leads to headaches, backaches, ulcers, chronic fatigue, general sickness, and other symptoms. An example will probably make this concept easier to understand. Tommy, a second grade student, is in the low reading group in his class and his classmates frequently make fun of his poor academic performance. Every morning, when it's time to go to school, he gets a negative signal. He knows, as young as he is, that school is not a satisfying place for him. His need for love is certainly unmet there, as well as his need for power since he is not as academically skilled as his peers. Tommy doesn't have much fun at school. He tells his parents that he doesn't want to go to school, but their answer is that he must go. This does not help Tommy satisfy his need for freedom. The negative signal is still going off loudly, urging him to try new behaviors to get what he wants. He tries crying and having a tantrum, behaviors that have been effective in the past. A power struggle with his parents ensues, but they still tell him that he must go to school. Tommy may give up the struggle, trying to ignore the signal, but as long as his needs are not being met, the signal will continue to work on Tommy. Soon, Tommy becomes sick. Now he can't go to school. Because his sickness is seen as something that just "happened" to him, Tommy gets lots of love, understanding, and support from his parents. One of them may even have to stay home from work to be with Tommy, providing him with an unexpected measure of power. Tommy is not being manipulative. He really is sick. If he were faking, it would likely be discovered and he would be sent to school. No one, including Tommy, realizes that the unaddressed negative signal still drives him to behave in an effort to satisfy his needs. The signal doesn't care if the behavior he chooses is irresponsible or harmful. The signal simply activates his system so that he will behave in an effort to satisfy his needs. Becoming sick is much more satisfying to Tommy than going to school and until he can find a better way to meet his needs in school, he will continue to be sick. There are thousands, maybe millions of children like Tommy who go through our school systems this way, missing an enormous number of school days. Most of them are completely unaware that their chronic inability to attend school is a creative behavior they have developed to help meet their needs.

If we want to keep our negative signals from becoming subversive and leading us into psychosomatic illness, we would be well advised to pay attention to them as soon as possible. We should practice recognizing negative signals before they get out of hand. We can help ourselves and our children to see negative signals more favorably. After all, negative signals provide us with the valuable information that we are not getting what we need. That information, if acted upon effectively and responsibly, can be a catalyst in our decision to live happier lives.

Although it is difficult to teach the concept of signals to young children, it is easy to recognize signals in children. As adults, we become skilled at masking our signals, and other people frequently are unable to read them in our body language or on our faces. Also, as we mature we choose more unique, individual patterns of behavior. You and I may both experience a negative signal, but show it in very different, subtle ways. Young children are more overt and demonstrative, as well as less individualized. Most preschoolers and primary grade students who experience strong positive signals show it in their faces immediately. Many of them get their whole bodies involved in the celebration, clapping, jumping, and laughing. Young children are just as quick to alert us when they have received negative signals. Crying, yelling, foot-stomping, and sulking are common behaviors among young children who have received negative signals. So while young children may have difficulty fully grasping the concept of signals, they can be taught to recognize the behaviors that quickly follow signals, both in themselves and in others.

The immediate goal, then, is to teach children to recognize the behaviors that accompany signals. The long range goal is to have children see that these behaviors are being chosen in an attempt to satisfy needs, and that other behaviors could be chosen, too. Put simply, while we don't choose the signal, we do choose what to do after we receive the signal.

Recognizing Positive Signals

Activity #1: Positive Signals

In this activity, Do-It introduces the concept of positive signals to children. Don't be surprised or alarmed if your children are unable to generate a long list for this activity. Since young children are still many years away from fully developing their individuality, their answers may represent a fairly narrow spectrum of behavior. As they get older, individual differences will become increasingly apparent. Here's a sample dialogue in which you and Do-It introduce positive signals to children.

You: (Keeping Do-It out of sight) Do-It? Oh, Do-It? Where are you? You said you'd be here when we wanted you. Do-It?

Do-It: (Popping up) Here I am! Just like I promised. It's important to do what you say you'll do. Hey, look at all those happy faces. That's just what I wanted to talk about.

Y: Happy faces?

D: Kind of. Remember when we talked before about what we need to be happy?

Y: Sure. Do you children remember? (At this point, briefly review the basic needs of love, power, fun, and freedom.)

D: My question for you now is, "How do you know when you're happy? How do you look? How could you tell, just by looking at someone, that he or she is happy?"

Y: I have an idea. Why don't we make another list. I've got some paper right here. Who wants to give Do-It some ideas about how we know when we're happy?

Record answers while Do-It interacts with the children. If younger children have difficulty, Do-It can ask such questions as: How do you look when you are happy? How do you feel when you get what you want? How does your body feel when you're happy? How can you tell, just by looking at someone, when he or she is happy? How did I know, just by looking at you, that you were happy to see me?

At the conclusion of the activity, make plans to have Do-It come again.

Activity #2: A Happy Book Activity

After completing the activity with Do-It, children can complete (with adult assistance) the page in *I'm Learning To Be Happy* titled "I Know When I'm Happy."

While the formal activities about recognizing positive signals are valuable, the real key to making this experience worthwhile is the regular follow-up provided by teachers and parents. First, practice being a model for the children. Tell them regularly how you feel and how your feelings are related to what you are doing. Secondly, each day, when you see children meeting their needs, ask them questions such as, "How do you know you're happy? What are you doing right now?" Children will gradually become skilled at recognizing the positive signals that indicate when their needs are being met. They will start to notice their smiles, their relaxed bodies, their faces free of tension. Ideally, you will help children make connections among their happiness, the responsible behaviors they choose, and their satisfied needs: "I'm smiling because I'm playing with Billy and having fun," "I'm clapping because I got it right!"

People who affirm and acknowledge that they are happy automatically become happier. I make it a point to bring my children's happiness to their attention regularly. I then help them identify the behaviors they have chosen. The connections they make between their behavior and their happiness makes it much more likely that they will be happy again soon. Happiness is no longer seen as something that just happens to them. They know when they are happy and what they did to be happy.

Activity #2: A Happy Book Activity

After completing the activity with Do-It, children can complete (with adult assistance) the page in *I'm Learning To Be Happy* titled "I Know When I'm Happy."

While the formal activities about recognizing positive signals are valuable, the real key to making this experience worthwhile is the regular follow-up provided by teachers and parents. First, practice being a model for the children. Tell them regularly how you feel and how your feelings are related to what you are doing. Secondly, each day, when you see children meeting their needs, ask them questions such as, "How do you know you're happy? What are you doing right now?" Children will gradually become skilled at recognizing the positive signals that indicate when their needs are being met. They will start to notice their smiles, their relaxed bodies, their faces free of tension. Ideally, you will help children make connections among their happiness, the responsible behaviors they choose, and their satisfied needs: "I'm smiling because I'm playing with Billy and having fun," "I'm clapping because I got it right!"

People who affirm and acknowledge that they are happy automatically become happier. I make it a point to bring my children's happiness to their attention regularly. I then help them identify the behaviors they have chosen. The connections they make between their behavior and their happiness makes it much more likely that they will be happy again soon. Happiness is no longer seen as something that just happens to them. They know when they are happy and what they did to be happy.

D: Kind of. Remember when we talked before about what we need to be happy?

Y: Sure. Do you children remember? (At this point, briefly review the basic needs of love, power, fun, and freedom.)

D: My question for you now is, "How do you know when you're happy? How do you look? How could you tell, just by looking at someone, that he or she is happy?"

Y: I have an idea. Why don't we make another list. I've got some paper right here. Who wants to give Do-It some ideas about how we know when we're happy?

Record answers while Do-It interacts with the children. If younger children have difficulty, Do-It can ask such questions as: How do you look when you are happy? How do you feel when you get what you want? How does your body feel when you're happy? How can you tell, just by looking at someone, when he or she is happy? How did I know, just by looking at you, that you were happy to see me?

At the conclusion of the activity, make plans to have Do-It come again.

If children experience difficulty, have Do-It ask them questions such as: How do you look when you are sad? How do you feel when you don't get what you want? How can you tell, just by looking, when another person is sad? After the list has been completed, continue your dialogue with Do-It.

Y: So what good is all of this, Do-It? How does knowing this help us to be happier?

D: Well, these things we've written down are just signals.

Y: Signals?

D: Yeah, signals tell us that we're not getting what we need.

Y: So?

D: Well, a lot of the time, what we're doing isn't helping us get what we want. Suppose you were playing with something and someone took it from you. What would you do?

Y: I might cry or look sad.

D: That's right. You get a signal that you're not happy, and then you do something like cry or look sad.

Y: But crying or looking sad doesn't usually help me get my things back.

D: That's right again. That's why whenever you get one of those negative signals you should stop and figure out what's wrong. Then plan to do something that will get you what you need without hurting anyone else.

Y: It sounds pretty tough to me.

D: It is. But we've got lots of time. For now, I just want you and the kids to practice recognizing signals. And we'll talk more later.

Y: O.K., Do-It. We'll practice recognizing our signals. See you soon.

What is most important in this activity is that you and Do-It help the children see that certain behaviors can alert them that they aren't meeting their needs. Think about why children typically cry, have tantrums, or otherwise show their unhappiness. Isn't this behavior always related to some unmet need? "They won't let me play with them" (love and belonging); "She took my block" (power); "I don't want to play that game" (freedom); "Can't we go down the slide one more time? Please?" (fun).

Our goal is to help unhappy children recognize and verbalize that they are getting a negative signal. At that point we can intervene and help them figure out a better way to get what they want. Once they realize that negative signals are trying to tell them something, even young children can begin to figure out how to behave more effectively. The cognitive benefit is that we are helping children overcome their tendency to behave impulsively. Instead of simply crying and continuing in their misery, we can introduce children to the idea that they need to do something else to meet their needs. That information alone is empowering and will help many children behave more effectively and responsibly.

Activity #4: Signals: Required Reading!

All of us will receive negative signals throughout our lives. One key to happiness is learning to recognize and use these signals to help us choose more effective behaviors. Begin by discussing the following important words with children: *behavior, negative,* and *signal.*

Behavior is made up of four components: acting, thinking, feeling, and physiology. (A detailed explanation of this concept is offered in Chapter Four: Behavior.) Remember to use vocabulary the children can understand. Rather than discuss "physiology," talk about what goes on in the body when we behave in certain ways. Children are quick to pick up this concept if you use examples like a tantrum, where the physiology of flushed face, tears, and body movement are easy to identify.

Talk about what the word *negative* means. Point out that negative behavior is behavior that will not help people become happier. I encourage you to explore with the children how "negative" information can be helpful. What would happen if we didn't receive negative signals? An example the children can probably understand is the negative signal we receive when we place our hand on a hot stove.

To introduce the concept of signals, compare them to signs with which they are familiar: Stop signs, their school sign, Railroad Crossing, etc. Just as these signs help us become more aware of what is happening in our world, negative signals warn us of potential danger. We need to learn to read these signs as well.

Discuss some of the negative signals children typically receive from their bodies when they are not meeting their needs and aren't happy. For example, the children may tell you "I am angry," "I feel like hitting someone," "I don't want to talk to anyone," or "sometimes I just feel like being mean." Each of these can provide the basis for healthy discussion that will promote responsible, pro-social behavior. Remember, too, that while they may not be able to control their negative signals, they always have control over what they do.

Just as children should talk about their negative signals, encourage them to talk about positive signals. Help them learn how their bodies feel when they are meeting their needs and feeling happy.

Activity #5: A Happy Book Activity

After discussing negative signals with Do-It, children can complete (with adult assistance) the page in their *I'm Learning To Be Happy* book headed "I Know When I'm Sad."

Activity #6: Mirror, Mirror!

This delightful group activity can be done just as easily at home with one child as it can in the classroom.

Have the children sit in a circle. Pass around a hand mirror and ask each child to make a "happy face," "sad face," "angry face," etc. Discuss with the children what they are doing when they feel happy, sad, angry, etc.

I know I'm sad when

_____

_____

_____

Activity #7: The Plate's The Thing!

This activity can be done equally well with a single child or a group. Give each child three plain white paper plates, and ask the children to draw a different face on each plate—one happy, one sad and one angry face. Then describe common situations and ask the children to hold up the plate that would represent the way they would feel in each. A discussion about the specific behaviors that accompany happiness, sadness, and anger could be included, geared to the developmental level of the children involved.

Chapter Three: Pictures

For each one of our basic needs, we have specific mental pictures or ideas of how we can satisfy that need. Each one of us develops our pictures individually, so mine will probably be different from yours.

While basic needs are universal, pictures are reflections of our individuality and are, in part, determined by our developmental level. A child's pictures might be something like these, developed by my son Greg when he was five years old:

Love: Me and my dad are at a baseball game.
Power: I hit a ball real far and get a home run.
Freedom: I decide what I want to do, like go to the park and play with my friends.
Fun: I am playing pirates or something like that with Kevin.

Throughout this book, I have spoken of wants. Our wants are usually represented in our brains as "pictures." These pictures are always related to our basic psychological needs. Everybody has pictures. Some of us have more than others, but every one of us has at least one picture of how we can satisfy each of our basic psychological needs. That doesn't mean that we can achieve the picture, that the picture is good for us, or that our pictures aren't in conflict with each other. Despite these potential trouble spots, we all have pictures.

We aren't born with pictures. We are born with needs, but virtually no idea how to satisfy them. As infants, we have very few behaviors we can perform voluntarily. Over time, however, certain behaviors we engage in satisfy our basic needs. We store away the accompanying experiences in our memories. As we get older, we add to our collection of pictures. Collectively, these pictures make up our Quality World—our individually developed notions of what is ideal.

Let's look at a couple of examples. Sarah, six months old, is alone in her crib and gets a negative signal, which means her needs are not being met. Like all infants, Sarah has very few behaviors she can voluntarily choose from to meet her needs. She begins to cry. Within minutes, perhaps seconds, her mother comes in, picks her up, and comforts her. Sarah quiets down and is a much happier infant. As young as she is, Sarah puts a picture in her tiny Quality World picture album of being held by her mother, a picture of satisfying her need for love and belonging that will probably stay there forever. While Sarah may not have sophisticated cognitive skills, you can be sure the event was significant enough that when she gets another negative signal in the near future, she'll most likely choose to cry because it has been proven effective in helping her meet her need for love and belonging.

Of course, crying, is not effective all of the time. When a behavior isn't effective, the negative signal continues to sound, and we search for other behaviors to meet our present needs. That's why, over time, Sarah will learn to satisfy her needs with behaviors other than crying. When those new behaviors produce a satisfying experience, that picture will be added to Sarah's Quality World.

The more pictures we have in our Quality World, the happier we'll be, because different pictures are effective in different situations. By having other pictures available we can still find ways to meet our needs. My son Greg told me that he wanted to play in the park with Kevin, but they couldn't because it was raining. Going to the park with Kevin was a picture he had in his head to satisfy the needs of love and fun. By having other pictures available, Greg was still able to meet his needs. He and Kevin played "investigator" with a magnifying glass, and later they played pirates. New pictures were substituted to meet the same basic needs.

Birthdays and holidays are times when many of us, including children, have very specific pictures of how we want our needs to be satisfied. Talking ahead of time about everyone's pictures is a good way to avoid much of the disappointment and conflict that can detract from these occasions. Discussing pictures ahead of time and working things out in advance also help us determine which pictures are really important and which ones we are willing to give up. A child may want to invite "everybody" to his birthday party. By telling him ahead of time that he can invite any five friends he wants, he has time to redevelop his picture and decide which of his friends are most important. As painful as these choices may be, the processes of discrimination and decision-making are very helpful as children come to understand their emerging value systems. If we, as adults, want to help children become effective decision-makers, it is helpful to provide them with opportunities to make decisions when they are young.

Remember, some pictures are not necessarily good for you in the long run, or even in the short run. Many children would prefer to eat candy instead of fruit, but we all know the different nutritional values of the two. Many children have a Quality World picture of watching TV and might do little else if their parents did not establish limits effectively. It is very difficult for children, who live for today, to consider the long-range implications of their behavior. That's where you, as a need-satisfying adult, become very important. If you become a picture in children's Quality Worlds, they are more likely to listen to you and accept fruit instead of candy, or play outside instead of watch TV. This strategy won't work all the time, but you can help children develop healthier pictures if you make yourself a need-satisfying person in their lives.

Unfortunately, pictures are not always compatible. One morning Greg was meeting his need for power as he built various structures with his blocks. He gets lots of recognition for the creative buildings he constructs. As soon as he was told that Kevin wanted him to come over to his house and play, a picture of being with his friend came into focus, which presented an opportunity to satisfy Greg's needs for love and fun. The two pictures could not be achieved simultaneously. A conflict, albeit minor, had to be resolved, so the blocks were put away for another time.

Through this process of resolving conflicts and making decisions, we construct our individual value systems and choose how to live our lives and what we will do in order to create happiness.

It is valuable to know just what your pictures are because they represent what you really want. Wanting something doesn't mean you will get it, of course; but if you can identify what you want and tell others what that is, you have a better chance of satisfying your wants and needs. Here is where teachers and other adults can be especially helpful to children. Remember that pictures relate to basic needs. When a child identifies a picture that he has, something he really wants, he's indirectly telling you what basic needs he wants to satisfy. Even if the picture he gives you is outlandish and can't be satisfied, you can still try to determine what needs the picture is designed to satisfy and help the child find other behaviors to satisfy those needs in the present.

If you want children to be really happy, you have to help them identify what they want and develop responsible behaviors that will turn those pictures into reality. Since many children have wants which can't be satisfied in the immediate future ("I want to be a Mommy," "I want to be on TV," etc.), focus on wants which they can satisfy in the present. For example, we may say, "You can pretend you are a Mommy and do the things a Mommy would do," or "We can get a video camera and you can practice what you want to do on TV." We are not trying to rob children of their dreams. Their long-range goals are critical components in their healthy development. Still, our immediate objective is to help children learn the process of choosing effective behaviors which will turn pictures into reality, and that process is more easily learned if we concentrate on short-term goals and objectives. The success children experience now will serve as a model to help them with bigger, long-range wants later in life.

Many adults fail to notice all the things they do well, the effective behaviors they use to achieve many of the pictures in their Quality Worlds. They constantly put more pressure on themselves, never believing they can slow down and relax. If you don't want your children to carry this psychological burden, help them affirm and appreciate all the things they do well to meet their needs.

The activities that are offered in this chapter involve considerable discussion. Young children need to be active and can only focus on discussions for short periods of time. Recognizing this, you may want to break these activities into smaller segments that can be spread over several days. It is not necessary to do an entire activity in one sitting, or even in one day. In fact, as a general rule, children profit from repetition. In all cases, use your judgment and move on to something else when you notice that the children are losing their concentration. Remember, we are trying to help children make the connection between behavior and happiness. They won't be able to do that without giving the activities their full attention and having fun.

Noticing What You Have

Activity #1: What We Have That Makes Us Happy

In this activity, Do-It will help the children recognize all the things they have that make them happy.

You: So, Do-It, what have you got planned for us today?

Do-It: Well, I've been doing a lot of thinking about this happiness thing.

Y: Yes, and what have you found?

D: It seems to me that the happiest people are more aware of all the things they have.

Y: What do you mean "aware"?

D: I mean they notice and appreciate all the things they *do* have instead of just complaining about what they *don't* have.

Y: And you think that makes people happier?

D: I'm sure of it. Everybody here has things that make them happy. Can we make another list?

Y: Sure. Let me reach over here and get the paper. Should we call it "What We Have That Makes Us Happy"?

D: Yes, that sounds good. Why don't you start us off with an example of something you have that makes you happy.

Y: O.K. I have friends. That makes me happy.

D: Good. Put that on our list. How about you kids? Let's hear some of the things you have that make you happy.

As Do-It and the children generate a list, you record their answers. At the completion of the activity, make plans to have Do-It come again soon.

Since children tend to be materialistic, you or Do-It might offer one or two ideas like "my family" or "my friends," but don't be alarmed if the children's list is disproportionately materialistic. That's probably a reflection of their developmental level. What's important is that children learn to be appreciative. If they can begin to learn that skill, then when they are older they will come to appreciate some of the more abstract things we cherish.

Activity #2: More of What Makes Us Happy

This activity is a wonderful way to spend the last fifteen minutes of the school day and I encourage you to do it at least twice a week. Before the children leave for home, talk about some of the things that happened that day which made the children feel happy.

Examples:

> In the classroom: "I finished all my math work!"
> In the gym: "I did great cartwheels on the mat."
> At lunch: "My favorite lunch was in my lunch box!"

These discussions help children develop a clearer sense of their Quality Worlds and increase their chances of creating their own happiness in the future.

Activity #3: Show and Tell

This activity has been a standard in classrooms for years and with good reason. Children have the opportunity to bring in a favorite book or toy and discuss it with the class. It is an affirmation of what represents quality in their lives and helps children understand their Quality Worlds more completely.

Activity #4: What We Have Done Right & What That Means

In this activity, Do-It will help children realize they have done many things right and have many positive qualities.

You: What are we going to do today to make us happy?

Do-It: Oh, I like that. "What are we going to do?" I think you're starting to learn that how happy we are depends on what we choose to do.

Y: So what's today's activity?

D: I thought it would be fun to spend more time talking about some of the things we already have.

Y: So we're going to do the same activity we did last time?

D: Not exactly. This time I want the kids to help me make a list called "What We Have Done Right And What That Means."

Y: Can you give us an example? I'm a little confused.

D: Sure. This is a tough activity. I met a kid once who told me "I learned to play Candy Land. That means I'm smart."

Y: I get it. Another child once told me, "I helped my Dad clean the kitchen. That means I'm a good helper."

D: That's a perfect example. Why don't we put those two on our list and now we'll hear from the kids. Who's got a good one for us to put on the list?

After the children have completed their list, make plans to have Do-It visit again soon.

Activity #5: The Job Jar

There are a number of routine jobs which need to be done at home or in the classroom which young children can do. List some of their favorite jobs on separate pieces of paper and place them in a jar. Each day, choose a couple of jobs which need to be done and let the children complete them. These experiences will help keep home or school in the children's Quality Worlds, and will help them satisfy their need for power in a healthy, responsible way.

Activity #6: My Kid Is a Big Help!

This is a wonderful activity to do in school or at home. Parents can write down ways in which their children are important and how they help out at home, then display the statement on the refrigerator or a wall. Teachers can do the same at school, writing down specific instances when children take on responsibility.

Activities #7 & #8: Happy Book Activities

The children can use the lists generated in Activities #1 & #4 to help them complete the appropriate pages in *I'm Learning To Be Happy* ("What I Have That Makes Me Happy" and "What I Have Done Right & What That Means").

WHAT I HAVE THAT MAKES ME HAPPY

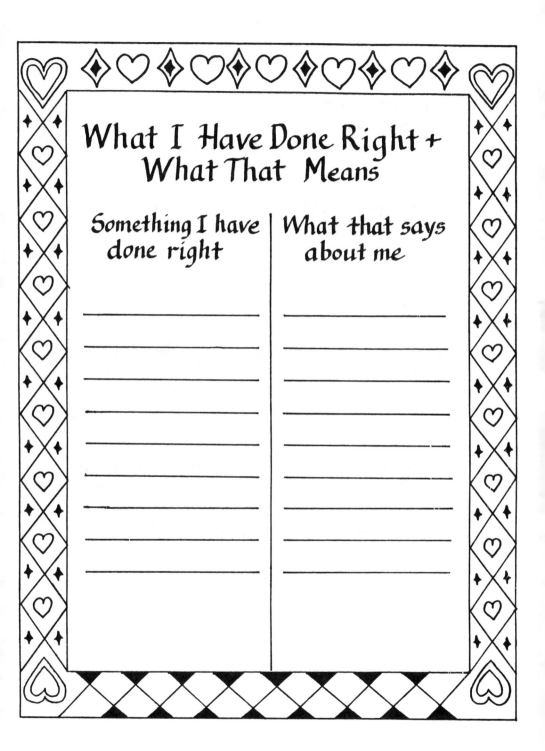

What I Have Done Right + What That Means

Something I have done right	What that says about me

Deciding What You Want

Activity #9: What We Want

Do-It will help the children create a list called "What We Want." Let the children use their imaginations, but encourage some easily obtained wants.

You: Good morning, Do-It. What have you got planned for us today?

Do-It: Dreaming.

Y: Dreaming?

D: Yep. We've been talking about all the things we have. Today, let's make a list of some things we would like to have.

Y: You mean like a new bike?

D: Sure. It could be a new bike. It could be just about anything. I'm sure the kids will help us with this one. I've never met a group of kids yet who couldn't tell me some things they would like.

Y: O.K., children. Who would like to go first?

At the conclusion of this activity, plan to have Do-It return.

Activity #10: Cloud Nine

This is a follow-up to the previous activity which you may want to return to again and again. Draw a large cloud on a piece of paper and duplicate it so that every child has one. The cloud will represent "Dreams," "My Quality World," or "How I Would Like Things To Be." Inside the cloud, the children can draw ideas, brainstorm words, or write stories, depending on the developmental level of the children. Topics might include the perfect weekend, when I grow up, my favorite foods, or my favorite activities.

When done in groups, this activity becomes a real opportunity to practice the skills of negotiation and compromise, since children rarely have the same Quality World pictures.

Activity #11: What We Have To Do To Get What We Want

Using the list that was developed in Activity #9, help the children divide their wishes into two groups: those that are relatively easy to get and those which will require more time and effort. With both lists, children should be encouraged to figure out what they have to do to make the wish come true. You may be surprised by the creative brainstorming abilities of the youngsters. Despite their limited experience, children can be incredibly creative, especially when it comes to figuring out how to get something they want.

Challenge the children. Ask them to imagine that they actually had this "want." How would their lives be different? In what ways would they be happier? Ask them if there would be anything bad about having this wish come true. You may need to point out logical consequences to three-year-olds. Many of them will be unaware of the dangers which might accompany some of their wishes. Still, with sufficient guidance and support, children age four and older can begin to appreciate the consequences of their behavioral choices.

Activity #12: Saying What You Want

The most honest and effective way to get what we want is to ask for it. We can help children learn how to ask for what they want in an appropriate way. This is an excellent opportunity to practice their ability to compromise and negotiate.

In this activity, let the children role play. Children love drama and this experience will help them practice important social skills. Here are a couple of samples:

A. Pretend you have invited a friend over for the day and now you discover that you want to do different things. How do you spend the day together and *both* be happy?
B. You are home with your family and everyone wants to watch TV. The problem is that everyone wants to watch something different and you only have one TV. How can you work it out?

Activity #13: A Happy Book Activity

Have children complete the "What I Have To Do To Get What I Want" page in their *I'm Learning To Be Happy* books, which ask them to identify three wants (at least two should be things they can get easily) and the behaviors they plan to use to make these pictures become reality.

What I Have To Do To Get What I Want

Some things I want	What I need to do
_____	_____
_____	_____
_____	_____
_____	_____
_____	_____
_____	_____

Activity #14: The Artist

Have the children paint or draw pictures of things that are in their Quality Worlds. Then ask the children about their art work and write their comments on the painting or drawing.

Activity #15: Building Happiness

At home or in school, have children use blocks to build something that makes them happy. Regardless of whether the children build farms, zoos, or entire cities, their creations represent a part of their Quality World.

Activity #16: Scrap Books

Parents and teachers can help children gather together photographs of happy times (birthdays, holidays, playing a favorite game, etc.) and place them in their own special scrapbooks. To make this activity even richer, have children dictate their descriptions of the significance of each picture and write their stories under each picture. This is especially valuable in a classroom based upon a whole language philosophy.

Activity #17: Pictures of a Quality Class

This activity may cost some money, but the impact it makes on the children makes the activity well worthwhile.

Keep a camera handy and take pictures of the children regularly as they are having fun and being productive in the classroom (doing a science experiment, playing a math game, working on an art project, etc.) Maintain a "Class Album," and label the pictures with a one or two sentence story.

This activity helps children keep "school," "teacher," and "learning" as need-satisfying pictures in their Quality Worlds. The same activity can be easily modified for home use, helping children to maintain the Quality World pictures of "home" and "family" in their lives.

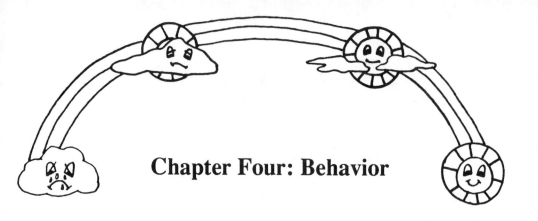

Chapter Four: Behavior

Just as our signals let us know if we are getting what we want, our behavioral system is working all the time to help us meet our needs. Our behavior is made up of four components, and all four parts are involved in every behavior in which we engage. These four parts are: acting, thinking, feeling, and physiology. Remember Sarah, the infant whose cries brought her mother? Most of us would identify Sarah's behavior as "crying," calling it by the most obvious of the four components that make up a total behavior. The crying was the acting part of Sarah's behavior. She may have been thinking that she wanted her mother or that she didn't want to be in her crib. Because of her age, her thoughts may not have been complex, but some type of thinking occurs in every total behavior. Feelings were also involved. Sarah may have felt lonely, sad, or frightened. If she hadn't been picked up promptly, feelings of frustration may have become part of the total behavior. Finally, every behavior involves physiology. In Sarah's case, the physiological component included the production of tears, a flushed face, and increased blood pressure. While most of us will probably continue to label behavior by its most overt or obvious component ("Tim's yelling." "Mary's depressed." "Becky's reading."), remember that in every total behavior there is acting, thinking, feeling, and physiology.

Most people have been trained to believe that they have no control over their feelings. In one sense, this is true. It's hard to start feeling cheerful when you are feeling depressed just by deciding to feel different. Still, we can significantly affect the way we feel if we remember that feelings are only one component of behavior. All four components work together all the time. We have the most control over our thoughts and actions. When we change these components of our total behavior, we also change how we feel. Therefore, we do have considerable control over our feelings, even though it's indirect control. If you want to feel better, do something different.

A truth many people find difficult to believe is that we choose all of our behaviors, even those which include unhappiness. We behave in an effort to get what we want. We could always do something else, so our behavior, though it becomes habitual, really is a choice. Accepting this fact ultimately empowers and liberates us as we realize that starting today we can make more effective choices, get more of what we want, and become happier people.

It is also important to remember that all of our behavior is chosen because, at the time, we believe that it represents our best chance to get what we want. All behavior, no matter how ineffective it is or how "stupid" it might appear to someone else, is done for a reason.

Even though all behavior is chosen, don't interpret that to mean it's easy to change. Behaviors become habits and habits are difficult to break. A child who has developed the habit of yelling in class instead of raising her hand will struggle as she tries to replace the yelling with new, more acceptable behaviors. The child who chooses an aggressive behavior when frustrated will encounter difficulty as he tries to substitute more appropriate choices for his aggression. To appreciate how automatic behaviors become and how difficult it is to break established patterns of behavior, try this experiment. Fold your arms across your chest. One hand is placed over the opposite arm and the other hand is tucked under its opposite arm. Now quickly fold your arms the opposite way! I'm sure many of you had difficulty changing this simple, value-free behavior. You probably felt awkward putting your hands and arms in the "wrong" position. The purpose of this experiment is to help you experience how difficult it is to change established, habitual behaviors. This doesn't mean you should not try to change behavior, but it does mean that you should not expect immediate, positive results with little effort. Setting realistic, achievable goals will make it easier for you to tolerate the slowness that accompanies most permanent, meaningful behavioral change. It will also make it easier for you to accept the slowness which accompanies meaningful change in the behavior of children.

Ineffective behaviors do not help you get what you want and frequently aggravate the situation. Effective behaviors help you get what you want in the long run and do not prevent the people around you from meeting their needs. Between ineffective and effective behaviors are a whole group of behaviors which are "band-aid" behaviors. In the long run these behaviors are ineffective, but they often appear effective because they provide us with short-term relief and trick us into believing that they are really helping us get what we need. Name calling, teasing, and scapegoating are typical band-aid behaviors that millions of children use, both at home and in school. These children feel better for the few minutes they are putting down another child. The behavior does address the need for power, but it also frustrates the need for love and belonging and is rarely helpful for very long. Many band-aid behaviors are correctly labeled "irresponsible" because they prevent others from satisfying their basic needs. While every one of us will continue to use ineffective and band-aid behaviors occasionally, with work we can increase our use of effective behaviors.

At this point, we should discuss a particular cluster of band-aid behaviors used by many people: aggressive behaviors. Aggressive behaviors are chosen by people in an attempt to satisfy their needs, frequently the need for power. Somewhat less obvious is the use of aggressive behavior to help satisfy the need for love and belonging. Many children want to be "friends" with the class bully, if for no other reason than to reduce their chances of being victims. To a lesser extent, aggressive behavior may also be chosen to help satisfy the needs for fun and freedom. Aggressive behaviors are not effective because they prevent other people from meeting their needs. Any behavior which interferes with other people's efforts to satisfy their needs is irresponsible and can never be considered effective. Our goal in working with young children is to help them develop a large repertoire of effective, responsible behaviors from which to choose. When we help young children learn to behave responsibly, we give them a better chance to live happy lives.

The effectiveness of any behavior depends upon how directly it addresses the unmet need which triggered the signal. If you acknowledge the signal, identify what you want in your life, and take effective steps to achieve that goal, then you will feel significantly better. If, instead, you merely recognize that you're unhappy and choose a behavior that makes you feel good, but does not directly address the unmet need, you will feel somewhat better, but not as good as you could feel. Let's suppose that Emily, an only child, gets a negative signal. The signal is trying to tell her that she currently needs more love and belonging, but there is no one available to play with her and both of her parents are busy right now. Emily's behavioral system comes up with the idea of working on a puzzle. She feels better because she is good at putting puzzles together, and the activity helps to satisfy her needs for power and fun. By changing the acting component of her total behavior, the feeling component also changed. Still, because Emily's choice did not directly address the unmet need for love that triggered the signal, she doesn't feel as happy as she could have if she had played with a friend or her parents. To be truly happy, it's critical to correctly interpret the message given to us by our signals and to find a behavior which allows us to satisfy the currently unmet need. This issue has particular importance for parents and teachers who redirect children when their behavior is disruptive or inappropriate. To be most effective, determine what need the child is attempting to satisfy with the disruptive behavior, then offer him an opportunity to engage in an appropriate activity that will address the same need. If a child is misbehaving in an effort to achieve power, and we engage him in a group activity which addresses the need for love and belonging, his disruptive behavior may diminish for a time, but he still will be driven by his unmet need for power and may soon become disruptive in the group. If, instead, we can involve him in an activity where he can meet his need for power responsibly, there is far less chance of his being disruptive. In short, redirecting misbehaving children can be an effective disciplinary strategy, but its effectiveness will be enhanced if the child is directed towards an activity that allows him to satisfy the unmet need which triggered the inappropriate behavior.

The objectives of the activities in this chapter are to help children learn the differences among ineffective, band-aid, and effective behaviors and to increase the number of responsible, effective behaviors available to help them meet their needs.

Activity #1: Different Kinds Of Behavior

Use Do-It to introduce the following dilemma to the children. Derek and Jason both want to play at one of the learning centers, but there is only room for one of them. Both receive internal signals, telling them that their needs are not being met. Here are some behavioral options available to these boys:

(1) *Ineffective:* Jason can walk away when Derek threatens to hit him if he doesn't get out of the way. Jason's behavior is ineffective because it does nothing to help him get what he wants.

(2) *Band-Aid*: Derek can threaten to hit Jason if he doesn't get out of his way. Derek's behavior appears effective as Jason moves away, but it is not responsible because it denies Jason the chance to satisfy his needs. Also, aggression is ineffective in the long run because Derek will ultimately lose his friends, thwarting his need for love.

(3) *Band-Aid:* Jason can cry when threatened by Derek. While Jason's behavior appears effective in the short run because it results in adult intervention, in the long run it doesn't help Jason meet his need for power or competence.

(4) *Effective:* Derek and Jason can agree to either take turns or both can wait until there is enough room at the learning center for both of them. These choices are effective because they allow both boys to meet their needs and there are no "losers."

Do-It will help the children begin to distinguish among ineffective, band-aid, and effective behaviors by discussing the examples above. Of course, children will have the most difficulty with band-aid behaviors because they give temporary relief and appear to be effective. The concept is especially difficult for children to master because they live in the present tense and have tremendous difficulty appreciating the long-range consequences of their behavioral choices. Many adults, too, confuse band-aid and effective behaviors, so don't be alarmed if your children have difficulty with this concept. Do-It can help the children by carefully questioning them about some of the possible negative consequences of using band-aid behaviors.

A key aspect of this activity is the process of brainstorming. With your help, children will come to realize that there's almost always more than one behavior to choose from, that they never "have to" do this or that, and that more effective behaviors can be chosen if they learn to take a minute to consider alternatives.

Here is a sample dialogue for this activity.

You: What's up for today, Do-It?

Do-It: Behavior, doing things. Remember last time we were talking about some of the things we would like to have?

Y: Sure, I remember.

D: Well, today we're going to talk about how we behave in order to get what we want.

Y: I hear lots of people talking about what they have to do to get what they want.

D: It's not easy, because some behaviors may help us get what we want but hurt other people. We don't want to do that because everybody has the same basic needs we've been talking about and it's not fair to make it hard for other kids to satisfy their needs.

Y: Would you give us an example, Do-It?

D: Sure. Let's imagine two boys, Derek and Jason. Both of them want to play at one of the learning areas in the room, but there's only room right now for one of them. There's lots of things they could do, right?

Y: Yes. I understand.

D: For example, Jason could just walk away if Derek threatens to hit him. Why isn't that a good choice for Jason?

Y: Because if he does that he won't get to play where he wanted to.

D: That's right. Whenever we choose a behavior that doesn't help us meet our needs, that behavior is ineffective.

Y: Are there other kinds of behavior?

D: Oh, sure. The trickiest is the next kind. These behaviors look like they help, but they usually only help for a while, not forever. Let me give you an example and see if the kids can figure out what the problem is.

Y: That sounds like fun.

D: O.K. This time, kids, pretend that when Derek tells Jason he's going to hit him, Jason cries and tells an adult. Will crying lead to other problems for Jason?

At this point, you, Do-It, and the children can discuss how Jason's crying makes it difficult for him to meet his need for power. Children may also concentrate on Jason getting a reputation as a cry baby and losing friends, frustrating his need for love and belonging. The critical issue here is that you help the children realize that Jason's behavior initially appears effective, but makes it difficult for him to satisfy his needs in the long run.

Y: So, Do-It, if that doesn't really help us, what should we do?

D:　The best kind of behaviors are called "effective." When you use effective behaviors, both you and the other person are able to get what you need.

Y:　Would you give us an example?

D:　I could, but let's see if the kids can figure out something Derek and Jason could do so that both of them are able to meet their needs. Does anyone have any ideas? Remember, both boys want to play at the same place, but there's only room right now for one of them.

Have the children offer Do-It suggestions for effective behaviors to resolve Derek and Jason's dilemma. During the discussion, be certain that Do-It offers some examples of effective behaviors if the children cannot come up with one independently. For example, Derek and Jason can agree to take turns or they can agree to wait until there's room for both of them. After discussing effective behaviors with the children, conclude the dialogue with Do-It.

Y:　Well, thanks, Do-It. We'll try to remember everything you told us.

D:　Good. The important thing to remember is that effective behaviors are the best, because they let everyone get what they need. And one more thing: you have to practice effective behaviors. It's not always easy, but you'll be glad you took the time to learn. Good luck, kids. I'll see you again soon.

Below is a list of challenging situations that young children typically encounter. In a group, have the children offer various suggestions about how to successfully meet these challenges. As always, the activities suggested here can be done individually, but this particular series of activities is especially well suited to group work because the children experience the process of brainstorming.

Try not to judge the suggestions as they are made and discourage the children from passing judgment before the list of suggestions is complete. Encourage creative solutions. It helps the children focus on the thinking component of total behavior. Also, the best, innovative solutions often grow from impractical, but creative ideas. After the list is completed, the children should decide if the solutions are ineffective, band-aids, or effective.

It is probably wise to discuss only one problem during a sitting. You can use the activity for several days in a row or come back to it periodically to review the concepts of ineffective, band-aid, and effective behaviors. Once the children have gone through this activity a couple of times, use actual problems that come up during the day. That would allow you to take advantage of real "teachable moments," and the problems would be much more interesting and relevant to the children since they would involve either them or their peers. Successfully resolving these issues would certainly add quality to the lives of the children.

(1) Katherine and Rachelle are on the only two swings in the playground. Meredith comes over and wants to join them. Katherine and Rachelle tell Meredith, "Go away. We're swinging and there's no room for you." Meredith leaves crying.

(2) Matthew is playing with blocks, not bothering anyone. Allen keeps knocking over Matthew's buildings and running away. Each time Allen does this, Matthew yells at him.

(3) Erika and Karen are best friends and like to play together. Today, as frequently happens, they are arguing about what game to play.

(4) Sam is having a wonderful time playing outside. When it is time to come in and listen to a story, Sam cries and complains that he doesn't want to come in, that he never gets to do anything he wants to do "in this dumb schoolhouse."

Activity #2: A Happy Book Activity

After working through the previous problems, children can choose a particular problem they would like to work on and then develop more effective solutions. Depending on the group, children may or may not be helpful to each other. Frequently it is easier to solve someone else's problem than it is to solve your own. This activity presents a wonderful opportunity to assist children in a positive way with some of the ineffective, disruptive behaviors they display. Encourage children to identify problems which they can overcome with relative ease. As the children gain practice in solving problems successfully, their self-esteem will improve. Later, they will be better equipped to tackle more difficult problem behaviors.

A Problem I Have:

_____

Some Solutions:

_____

_____

_____

_____

"A Problem I Have & Some Solutions" in *I'm Learning To Be Happy* can be used to identify a problem and some responsible, effective behaviors a child could use to solve it. (When a child successfully overcomes a problem, it gives you the opportunity to add "overcomes problems" to the child's "Things I Do Well" page, a wonderful way to build self-esteem.)

Activity #3: Role Plays

If the children continue to have difficulty choosing effective behaviors you can use role-playing as a way to help them practice the concepts that were taught in the previous activity. Several ideas are provided to get you started. Feel free to develop your own appropriate role play situations which will give children the chance to practice behaving in an effective, responsible fashion. To make this activity valuable, take time to discuss the role plays with children when they are finished. Talking about what makes some behaviors better than others is critical in helping children build a repertoire of effective behaviors.

(1) You and your brother can't agree on which show to watch on TV. Role play showing ineffective and effective behaviors.

(2) There is only one piece of pie left when you and your sister arrive home from school. It's your favorite and hers, too. Role play, demonstrating ineffective and effective behaviors.

(3) At recess, the class is breaking into teams to play a game. Neither side has picked you. Role play some ways you could behave, showing ineffective and effective behaviors.

Note: Remember that understanding the concept of band-aid behaviors is difficult for young children. If you believe that the children you deal with would not understand the concept sufficiently, it is enough to have them role-play and learn about the difference between ineffective and effective behaviors.

Activity #4: Effective Behaviors

This is a wonderful brainstorming activity which will help the children come up with a host of effective behaviors they can utilize in a variety of situations. Choosing topics appropriate to your particular circumstances, have the students cooperatively develop lists of effective behaviors to deal with situations like those listed below:

1. making a friend
2. doing quality work in school
3. getting along well with parents and other family members
4. enjoying time with your friends
5. improving a _____ (sports, reading, science, musical) skill.

Activity #5: There's Always A Choice

Anyone who works with young children has had the experience of hearing them defend their misbehavior by insisting, "I couldn't help it" or "He made me do it." In this activity, children will be invited to explore more effective options and begin to learn that they always have some control over what they do.

Have children complete the following sentences:

When I feel angry I usually _____, but I could _____ instead.

When I am lonely I usually _____, but I could _____ instead.

When I am scared I usually _____, but I could _____ instead.

Chapter Five: Balance

If you aren't currently meeting all of your basic psychological needs (love, power, fun, and freedom) in a balanced, responsible way, you are not as happy as you could be. Since we meet our needs by interacting with others and engaging in various activities, one key to happiness is to make sure that we have enough people and activities in our lives to meet all of our needs effectively.

The most successful early childhood education programs emphasize the concept of balance. You can take a first step toward increasing the effectiveness of your program if you take time to evaluate the activities you currently use and determine what needs they address. Even if your program is filled with wonderful, satisfying activities, you may discover that it lacks balance. Don't be surprised, for example, if you find your program lacks enough activities which help children satisfy their needs for power and freedom. Once you have done an assessment of your current activities, you can begin to supplement your program with activities that address any deficits you discover.

Parents, too, can use the concept of balance in dealing with their children at home. Make sure you give your children not only love, but opportunities to meet their needs for power, fun, and freedom. Simple ways to help children meet their need for power are to help them become as self-sufficient as possible and to engage in meaningful work within the home. Being responsible for simple household chores helps a child become responsible, builds self-esteem, and helps satisfy the need for power. Giving children choices and making them aware that they do make choices helps them meet their need for freedom. A choice can be as simple as letting your child decide which of the two bedtime stories you have approved will be read. Such an approach satisfies the child's need for freedom while simultaneously establishing reasonable perimeters.

As difficult as it is for adults to achieve balance in their lives, it is even more difficult for children. Young children have the same needs that we have, but don't have the same capacity to satisfy their needs, especially their need for power. Remember, too, that each of us has our own Quality World pictures of how we want to satisfy our needs, and the pictures of young children are quite different from the pictures of adults. Listen to a typical two-year-old for awhile. That unequivocal "No!" and "Me do it!" and "No like that one!" that you hear are all strong declarations that even very young children are motivated by the need for power and are just as driven to satisfy their needs. You may never witness greater focused motivation and determination than when you observe a five-month-old struggling for an out-of-reach toy, or a nine-month-old struggling to pull herself up in the crib, or a thirteen-month-old falling again and again as he learns to take his first steps across the room. All of these struggles are undertaken to establish competence, to gain recognition, and to satisfy the inborn need for power.

Think about all the "misbehavior" children engage in at school to meet their need for power. If we were to develop activities which would allow them to satisfy the need for power within teacher-sanctioned activities, they would be less driven to misbehave in class. In our early childhood education programs we have done a wonderful job of creating environments where children can meet their needs for love and fun. We have been less successful, however, in creating environments where children can meet their needs for power and freedom. The consequence of this is the misbehavior which diminishes the effectiveness of many otherwise high quality programs.

Let's look at two examples of children who are good at meeting some of their needs, but lack balance in their lives.

Kristin is a four-year-old, living with both her parents in an upper middle class suburb. An only child, Kristin is showered with love, attention, and gifts by her parents and other relatives. She attends a preschool program three days a week and is well liked by the other children in the program. Her teachers find her somewhat "immature," but very compliant and easy to manage. Kristin plays actively and gets along well with her classmates. Despite all this, Kristin's life is not in good balance because she doesn't have enough opportunities to meet her need for power.

Ever since Kristin was an infant, her parents, both well educated, have done everything to make Kristin "the happiest little girl in the world." In the process, Kristin has never had to struggle for anything, and any time her parents have seen her even slightly frustrated, they have come to her rescue. Her self-help skills are underdeveloped, and Kristin has had very few opportunities to develop the self-esteem necessary to satisfy her need for power. Because Kristin is well cared for and her parents are well intentioned, it's difficult for people to realize that she is a young girl who is less happy than she could be because her life is not in balance. If we were to visualize a circle of Kristin's basic needs, it would look like this:

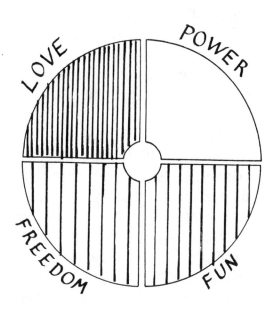

Jeffrey is in the third grade. His mother, a single parent, is a very serious woman who has impressed upon Jeffrey the importance of "paying attention and not fooling around in school." Many of the people who live in their neighborhood are out of work and have had minimal education. Jeffrey's mother is determined that her son "will not become like them. He's going to make something of himself and will not be dragged down by any bad influences." Jeffrey is rarely allowed to accept invitations to other children's homes and his mother keeps visits from other children to a minimum. Jeffrey does very well in school and shows signs of being academically gifted. Still, he interacts very little with his classmates and appears sullen and withdrawn much of the time. Since Jeffrey gets good grades in school and his mother acknowledges his achievements, he is meeting his need for power. His relationship with his mother helps him meet his need for love, although he is somewhat deprived in this area because he has such limited access to friends. Jeffrey makes choices every day, but is still restricted by his mother, so his need for freedom is not adequately met. The most glaring unmet need for Jeffrey, however, is fun. Despite, or perhaps because of, his mother's good intentions, Jeffrey has been asked to be much more serious and cautious than most third grade students, and he has had very few opportunities to have fun. Jeffrey's Basic Needs Circle might look like this:

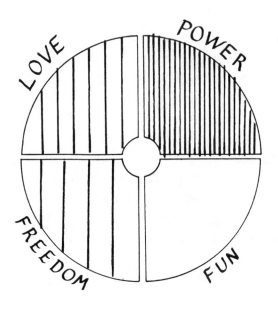

Despite the strengths that both Kristin and Jeffrey have, neither child is as happy as possible because their needs are not satisfied in a balanced way. Remember to experience happiness regularly, we must satisfy each of our basic needs in a balanced way on a daily basis.

Balancing Your Needs

Activity #1: Basic Needs Circle

This is a fun activity which should offer you a view of how successfully your children are balancing their needs. You may find this activity helpful if you are dealing with children who don't seem particularly happy, and you haven't been able to figure out why. Their comments during this activity may help both you and the children realize what need or needs are not being met.

The objective of this activity is to have children complete a Basic Needs Circle. Begin by having Do-It help the children generate a list of important people and activities in their lives. Remember, we satisfy our needs by interacting with others or by engaging in activities either alone or with others. As usual, it may be advantageous to begin this activity as a group, but this is not necessary.

You: Good morning, Do-It.

Do-It: Hi, everybody.

Y: What's that you've got with you?

D: This? (Showing a Basic Needs Circle) This is a Basic Needs Circle.

Y: What's it for?

D: Remember the basic needs we keep talking about?

Y: Sure. Love, power, freedom, and fun, right?

D: That's right. Well, this circle has a space to help us figure out how we meet each of these needs. Here's one for love. Here's one for power. Here's fun. And here's freedom.

Y: But there's nothing on it.

D: I know. That's why I came. I was hoping the kids would help me fill out a Basic Needs Circle. Would you kids be interested in helping me?

If this activity is done in a group setting, it is wise to make a "group" Basic Needs Circle. It will draw on the strengths of many children. You will end up with a balanced circle, and the kids will all experience the process of completing the Basic Needs Circle. The activity, of course, can also be done individually.

D: O.K. Let's start with people. Can you think of someone who really loves you, even if they sometimes get angry with you?

Do-It should take a few names from children and you can list them in the "Love" quadrant of the Basic Needs Circle.

D: Let's do this section called "Power." Can you think of someone who tells you that you do things well? Someone who thinks you've got some good ideas?

Do-It will get the names of several people for you to list in the "Power" quadrant.

D: Great job! Now let's do the section that says "Fun." Who is a person you like to play with? Someone who makes you laugh? Who helps you learn new things?

Again, Do-It will choose a few names for you to include in the "Fun" quadrant. If the activity is being done in a group, have Do-It call on a variety of children so that everyone feels involved and important.

D: O.K., kids. The last section of the circle says "Freedom." Who are some people who let you make choices, who let you make some decisions about what to do?

Y: Thanks, Do-It. We have a nice circle filled with people who help us satisfy our needs.

D: But we're not finished yet! We meet our needs through people and activities. We still need to list the things we do to help us meet our needs. Come on, kids. Let's start with love again. Who can think of something that you do that makes you feel like you're part of a club or group?

D: O.K., now let's talk about power. Someone tell me something you do well. . .

D: Great. Let's talk about fun. Let's think of some things that are really fun to do, things you enjoy doing. . .

D: And now let's talk about freedom. What is something that you do where you get to make choices and decisions? . . .

D: Now we've got it! This is a beautiful Basic Needs Circle that includes lots of the people and activities that help you meet your needs. I'm glad we did this. After I leave, maybe each of you can make your own Basic Needs Circle, just for you!

Y: Thanks, Do-It. I think we'll want to do that someday soon.

D: I'd like to see them when they're finished. Remember to have fun when you're doing it! See you soon!

Activity #2: A Happy Book Activity

After children have finished answering Do-It's questions about each important person and activity, they are ready to complete the Basic Needs Circle contained in *I'm Learning To Be Happy*. Each person and activity

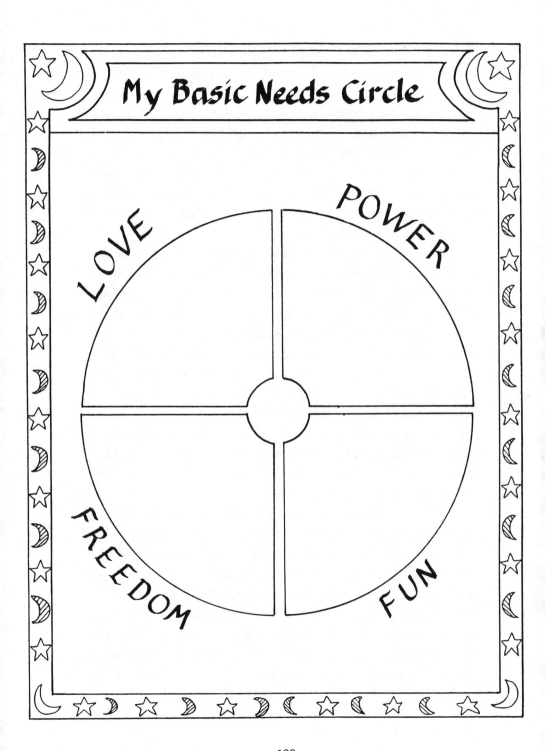

should be considered separately to determine what needs are met. If a person helps a child meet all of her needs, list them in each quadrant of the Basic Needs Circle. On the other hand, if a person helps a child meet only one or two needs, list that person only in the appropriate quadrant(s). When each child has finished this activity, you will have completed a Basic Needs Circle for each child which identifies the people and activities important to them in their attempts to meet their needs. It is literally a visual representation of their Quality World.

The Basic Needs Circle is useful for two reasons. First, as an adult, you can quickly identify children whose needs are not balanced when you see one or two quadrants which are empty or close to empty. Secondly, the Basic Needs Circle is important for you and the children because it identifies, in specific terms, how the children go about satisfying their needs. This will come in handy when children get negative signals and have trouble figuring out what to do to feel happier. It's not always easy to figure out what to do when you're feeling down. By completing the Basic Needs Circle, however, you and the children can refer to it and identify people and activities that have been sources of happiness in the past.

The real value of this activity will be determined by how honestly the children answer your questions. Some children, both because they want to please and because they may have difficulty understanding some of the concepts involved, may give answers that aren't helpful. For example, if Matthew doesn't usually play with Randy, on the one day the two boys happen to play together you may be given distorted information. Matthew may make it seem as if Randy helps him satisfy all of his needs when, in fact, the truth is very different. You will have to use skill and the power of discrimination to help children create a truly valid Basic Needs Circle. Instead of relying solely on the information the child provides during the activity, be certain to use what you have observed and what you know about the child to help you.

To help get you started, here's an example of a Basic Needs Circle, thanks to my children:

Maintenance

Activity #3: A Happy Book Activity

Whether children's Basic Needs Circles reveal balance or not, the objective now is to build on whatever strengths they currently have. (There will be time later for them to create better balance in their lives.) The first step is to help them maintain those things they currently do which help them satisfy their needs. Too often, we pay more attention to our problems than we do to the successes we already have. Emphasizing our deficits does little to help our self-esteem, and failure to recognize and maintain our strengths can result in losing those skills we do have. This

KEEPING UP the GOOD WORK

In order to continue _____

I will _____

In order to continue _____

I will _____

In order to continue _____

I will _____

activity is designed to help children recognize what they already have and to help them practice behaviors which have been successful for them in the past.

Children should do this activity individually, with adult assistance, using the Basic Needs Circles they have completed. You can use Do-It to help you with this activity if you want. The "Keeping Up The Good Work" page in *I'm Learning To Be Happy* asks children to identify things from their Basic Needs Circle which they would like to maintain.

It is important for children to realize that good things exist in their lives because of behaviors they choose. If they want to continue experiencing the happiness they currently enjoy, help them identify specific behaviors they can use to continue meeting their needs.

Children can be remarkably vague in their description of behavior. Encourage them to be specific when completing this activity. For example, "I will be his friend" is not nearly as helpful as "I will make sure to invite him to play a game with me." Also, encourage the children to identify issues and behaviors which they can do easily and regularly. Having successful experiences will help build their self-esteem.

Activity #4: Make a Mobile

Have children make a mobile by crossing two straws and hanging yarn from each of the ends. On each of four 3"x5" index cards write one of the basic needs (love, power, fun, and freedom). As you help the children attach their cards to the yarn, show them that their mobiles aren't balanced unless all of the cards (needs) are hanging on the mobiles. In the center of each mobile, hang a card with the child's name on it. The mobile represents the child, balanced by all four needs.

Activity #5: Expand the Mobile

After completing the previous activity, ask the children to write on index cards the names of people and activities which help them satisfy each of their basic needs (one person or activity per index card). The cards should be labeled according to the need satisfied by that particular person or activity. Children can then hang these index cards on their mobile under the corresponding need and actually see how balanced their lives are.

Activity #6: Balancing Our Needs At School

The following suggestions are offered to teachers who want to make sure that students meet their needs in school in a balanced way.

Love:
1. Structure academic activities in cooperative groups.
2. Allow children to sit close to friends, provided that they do quality work.
3. Have cooperative groups give themselves a name, enabling them to develop a stronger sense of belonging.
4. Teach children about "encouraging statements" and support them when you hear them being used in class. (encouraging statements are phrases such as "good work," "nice picture," "interesting story," etc. Display statements such as these on the walls so the children can use them as models as they encourage their peers.)

5. If possible, let the class have a pet, and discuss the importance of having pets as a way to meet our need for love and belonging.

Power:
1. Assign work which you believe the students can do well.
2. Expect quality work and make it realistically attainable by all.
3. Be certain that activities and learning centers are varied so that every child has an opportunity to shine.
4. Introduce new concepts first to the whole class, then let children work in small groups. Finally, let children work independently. This method gives children exposure to different teaching and learning styles before being asked to perform on their own.
5. Have children evaluate their own work for quality instead of relying exclusively on an evaluation by the teacher.

Freedom:
1. Whenever possible, give children choices regarding assignments . For example, everyone may need to read a book about dinosaurs, but you may offer them fifteen books from which to choose.
2. Let the class develop the schedule for the day when possible.
3. Let the class pick the story to be read to the group.
4. During physical education, list three games and let the children decide which game is to be played.
5. In general, give as much freedom as you can. The more freedom you give to children, the more

willingly they will do what you ask them to do, even if it is not immediately need-satisfying.

Fun:
1. If you have followed the suggestions given so far, you can be reasonably certain your children are having fun. Congratulate yourself! Remember to keep photographing these activities and discussing them as much as possible. The more children talk about their Quality World and their need-satisfying experiences, the more they will develop a sense of internal control.

Chapter Six: Options

As adults we recognize the importance of having many options from which to choose. When I went to college, my parents encouraged me to take enough education courses to become certified as a teacher "just to keep your options open." Options are just as important for children. My son Greg loves music, and at the age of three he announced that he wanted to play the cello. When he turned four, my wife and I signed him up for lessons, but Greg was told that he was too small to play a cello and would have to begin with a violin. Because Greg was able to switch Quality World pictures quickly (he only chose misery for a short time and decided it wasn't particularly satisfying), he has been able to pursue his love for music and now finds that playing the violin satisfies his needs for love, power, and fun. If he hadn't been flexible, Greg would have missed a chance to create happiness for himself. Quite simply, options give us more opportunities to satisfy our needs and experience happiness.

It is critically important for all of us, even young children, to develop options to help us meet our needs. If Laura only feels a sense of power when she is painting and her painting class is canceled, she will be in trouble. Her need for power will be as strong, but she will no longer have any behaviors she can use to meet this need. Similarly, if Tim experiences fun only when he is swimming and he has limited swimming opportunities, he will still be driven to satisfy the need for fun but will often have no behaviors available to help him meet his need.

Options can provide us with different ways to meet our goals. As adults, we know that things don't always turn out exactly as we had hoped. Our task is to take things as they are and find a way to satisfy our needs. Think of it as developing as many pictures as possible to expand our Quality Worlds. This way, if something goes wrong and one of our pictures is no longer attainable, we still have other pictures to satisfy our needs. This doesn't mean that we don't feel the loss we have suffered. However, we choose not to be paralyzed by that loss, and instead choose to be as happy as we can be.

Children need to develop options too. If Melanie is only going to meet her need for love and belonging by being with someone in her immediate family, she's going to be miserable at school. While it's likely that her family members will always remain prominent pictures for her, she will have to develop acceptable alternatives if she's going to be happy at school. If Greg has a Quality World picture of meeting his need for fun by playing the board game Sorry and he can't find the game, it would be helpful if he could substitute another game as a picture to satisfy this need. If Kristy has a picture in her head of dancing to satisfy her need for power, and ultimately decides she is not talented enough to pursue dancing as a career, she will still have a need for power. Kristy will be a happier adult if she develops alternative pictures, perhaps teaching dance to young children.

We help children tremendously when we teach them at the earliest possible age to develop acceptable options. Children should be encouraged to think of many ways to satisfy their needs. Just as importantly, they should engage in a variety of behaviors so they can experience alternative ways to meet their needs for love, power, fun, and freedom. The more options they have available, the more resilient they are, and the happier they will be. Children benefit from being taught options because it gives them a greater sense of control over their lives. They are more willing to accept responsibility for their own happiness if they have been given the skills to create it effectively, responsibly, and regularly.

It is probably easier to teach options to young children than to adults. Adults tend to have their Quality World pictures very much in focus, know exactly what they want, and are less likely to settle for alternative pictures. Many adults actually choose to be miserable, at least for a while, rather than accept another picture. Children are generally more flexible. If Greg wants Eric to come over to play and Eric isn't home, Michael or Will are usually acceptable substitutes. The joy of teaching options to young children is that it is easy and gives them the message from a very early age that there are a variety of ways to satisfy their basic needs. If one pathway is blocked, another pathway can be found. As was discussed in Chapter Four, behaviors become habits. Exercising your options is one habit you'll be glad you developed.

Remember, every one of us, young and old, must satisfy all of our needs every day to be happy. The more options we create for ourselves, the more happiness we will experience.

Creating A Balanced Basic Needs Circle

Activity #1: A Happy Book Activity

In many ways, the chapter on balance is the central chapter in this book, since balancing our needs is critical to experiencing happiness. This activity is designed to help children who don't have sufficient balance develop some alternatives and meet their needs more effectively.

Look at the "Adding Balance To My Basic Needs Circle" page in *I'm Learning To Be Happy*. Each quadrant of the Basic Needs Circle is divided into two sections: one for people and activities which the child already has, and one for people and activities the child could add to create more options and better balance. With your help, children can complete the "Have" section by copying their completed Basic Needs Circle from the earlier page. You may use Do-It to work with the children on this activity.

Adding Balance To My Basic Needs Circle

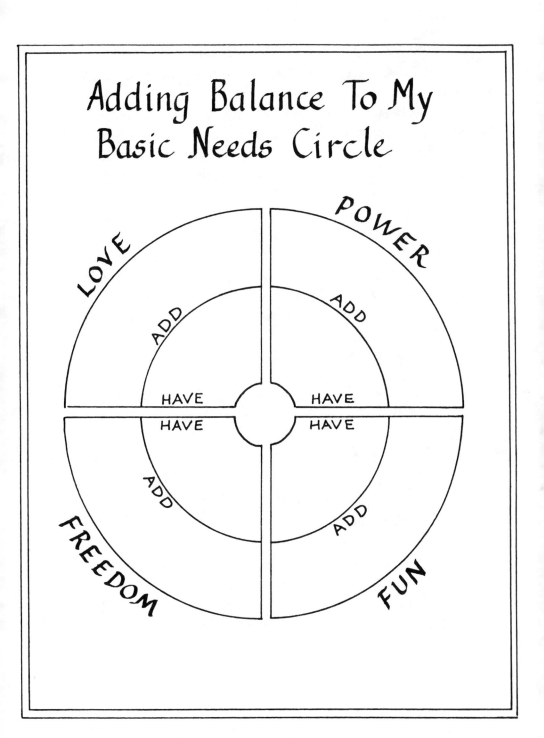

Activity #2: Things We Would Like To Add

In this activity, Do-It assists the children as they complete the "Add" section of the Basic Needs Circles they have been working on in *I'm Learning To Be Happy*. The "Add" section can be approached in several ways. Children can work on this activity individually with help from you and Do-It. It is also possible for children to share their Basic Needs Circles with each other so that they can get new ideas that they may want to add to their own Basic Needs Circles. Or some type of combination approach could be used to complete the activity. Regardless of which approach you choose, all the children should end up with specific people and activities which they can add to their lives to satisfy their needs effectively and in a more balanced way.

Do-It can discuss some of the options outlined below with the children. This will help them see that there are various possibilities available to include in the "Add" section of their Basic Needs Circles. A sample dialogue follows.

Where To Look To Create More Love & Belonging In Your Life

▲ Is there another child in my class or neighborhood I would like to get to know better?

▲ What are things I like to do? Are there other children who would like to do these things with me?

▲ Can I take part in any activities where I can meet other children? (arts and crafts, music, play group, sports, etc.)

Where To Look To Create More Power & Recognition In Your Life

▲ I get power and recognition for the things I do well. What are some of the things I do well now? (read, ride a bike, know my colors, etc.)

▲ What are some of the things I could learn to do to get more power and recognition? (play a new game, get dressed all by myself, learn to spell more words, etc.)

Where To Look To Create More Fun & Pleasure In Your Life

▲ I have lots of fun when I learn new things. What new thing could I learn?

▲ When was the last time I heard a joke? Bought an ice cream cone? Made popcorn & watched a movie with my family? Went to the park? Went on a picnic? Went someplace special with my family?

Where To Look To Create More Freedom In Your Life

▲ People are free when they make decisions. What are some of the decisions I have made today? (what to wear, what activity to do in school, what to eat for lunch, etc.)

▲ People get freedom by making things. What is something I can make today that would help me feel free? (a model airplane, a drawing, a pinwheel, etc.)

▲ I feel more free when I move. When am I going to dance so I can feel more free?

▲ Even though I'm still young, I need free time, too. Starting now, I'm going to have some time every day when I can do whatever I want to do as long as it doesn't hurt anybody and doesn't break any rules.

Sample dialogue with Do-It:

Do-It: Good morning, kids. I hear you have all been working on Basic Needs Circles.

You: That's right, Do-It, we have. The children have already completed the "Have" sections of their circles and now we're going to work on the "Add" sections. Would you like to help?

D: I'd be delighted. O.K., kids, please take out your Basic Needs Circles. See where it says "Love"? It looks like you've got some people and activities there already. Now let's think about other people you want to be friends with, or games you could play, or places you could visit to meet even more people. Who can suggest something?

Include some of the suggestions made by the children in the "Add" section of the "Love" quadrant. Continue to list suggestions in the other quadrants as Do-It asks for them.

D: Great. Let's add to the "Power" section. Can anyone think of something they could learn to do well to get more recognition?

D: How about the "Fun" section? Learning is fun. What are some new things you could learn? What are some other fun things you would like to add to your circles?

D: And let's not forget about the "Freedom" section. What are some ways you could add more freedom and more choices to your life?

D: Wow! Look at that Basic Needs Circle now! Not only do you have lots of things already, there are a whole lot of things you can add to your lives to make them even happier.

Y: Thanks for helping, Do-It.

D: It was my pleasure. Thanks, kids. I'll see you again real soon.

Start Adding Happiness Now

Activity #3: Do-It Helps Make a Plan

The first two activities in this chapter were designed primarily to help children think about balancing their needs more effectively. Our ultimate goal, however, is to help children actively create their own happiness, not simply think about creating it. The objective of Activity #3 is to translate the thinking done in the previous activities into a specific plan of action. Do-It leads a discussion about some of the things children included in the "Add" sections of their Basic Needs Circles. Then the children choose one issue to work on collectively and brainstorm with Do-It about what they need to do to get what they want. At the end of the activity, Do-It will have taken the children through the process of developing a specific plan to add more happiness to their lives. Here's a sample dialogue to show you how the discussion might go.

You: Good morning, Do-It. You seem especially happy this morning.

Do-It: I am because I have something special to tell the kids. Are you going to ask me what it is?

Y: Sure, Do-It. What do you have planned for today?

D: Well, you know how we've been working on our Basic Needs Circles?

Y: Of course I do.

D: Well, today I want to talk about how we can actually have some of the things we put in the "Add" sections of our Basic Needs Circles!

Y: That sounds exciting.

D: It is. Let's get going. Can I have a volunteer?

The remaining dialogue is for illustration only, as each child will have different things in the "Add" section of the Basic Needs Circles. For this illustration, I have chosen something many children would like to have—another friend.

Y: I think Valerie has something she would like to add to her Basic Needs Circle.

D: O.K., Valerie. Let's see what we can do. What do you have in the "Add" section that you would really like to work on so you can put it in the "Have" section?

Valerie: Well, Do-It, I have lots of things.

D: Good, Valerie. That shows that you've been thinking. Before we pick one, remember that you'll have to do some work. You can't have things just by wanting them. It has to be something you're willing to work for.

V: Well, Do-It, I have lots of friends, but I'd like to have even more because sometimes my friends are sick or busy and I have no one to play with.

D: O.K. If you want another friend, what can you do?

V: I can wait for someone to invite me to their house to play.

D: Sure, but suppose they don't invite you, even if you wait for a long time?

V: Then I'll be sad.

D: Waiting for someone else to do something is not the best way to be happy. Someone may invite you because you are very nice, but then again, they might not invite you. So what can *you* do to make another friend?

V: I could invite someone to my house to play!

D: Have you thought of who you would want to invite?

V: I'm not sure yet.

D: Then let's do some planning. Who would you most like to add to your list of friends?

V: I think I would pick Robin.

D: O.K. When would you like to have Robin over to play?

V: Today!

D: Have you asked your Mom?

V: Oh, I forgot about that. Well, tomorrow would be OK.

D: When will you ask your mother?

V: Today. After school.

D: Suppose she says tomorrow is a busy day and Robin can't come over then?

V: Then I'll ask her if we can do it another day. And, after I ask my mother, I'll make plans with Robin.

D: Great, Valerie. That's how you can move something or someone from the "Add" section to the "Have" section of your Basic Needs Circle.

Y: Thanks, Do-It. I think all the children will want to make plans, just like Valerie did.

D: Great! That's what being in control of your own happiness is all about. Just remember, kids, that making plans takes time and work. Make sure you plan carefully so you can really get more of what you want. That's why it's a good idea to have a grown-up help you plan. And if a plan doesn't work as well as you'd like, you can always make a different plan. It's like that old saying: if at first you don't succeed, try, try again! Well, good luck and happy planning! I'll see you all soon.

Activity #4: A Happy Book Activity

Children are to choose one of the people or activities they have listed in the "Add" section of their Basic Needs Circles, then decide exactly what they will do to move that person or activity from "Add" to "Have" on their Basic Needs Circle. Of course, children will need your help to plan specific, effective behaviors, but it is important for them to learn that if they want to be happier, they have to do something different. By completing the "Do It" page in *I'm Learning To Be Happy*, children will develop a specific plan to add more balance to their lives. Again, you are urged to help children choose wisely. Their choices should be attainable so they will have satisfying experiences that enhance the balance in their lives and help them learn that they are capable of creating their own happiness.

DO IT

So I can have:

_____

I need to:

_____

_____

_____

Chapter Seven: Relationships

Since we frequently meet our needs interacting with other people, the quality of our personal relationships is an important consideration in our effort to live happy lives. We need other people in our lives to help us meet our needs, but frequently we find ourselves in conflict with them.

Often the conflict is due to our different Quality World pictures. Suppose Becky asks Aaron if he wants to do something fun and he agrees. At that moment, each of them has a perfectly developed Quality World picture of what "fun" with the other will be. Becky might envision sitting down and playing a favorite board game. Aaron's Quality World pictures might involve riding bikes and searching for a buried treasure. Ultimately, the success of the relationship depends upon the ability of the people involved to work things out so that both are able to satisfy their needs. If they are unable to do this, either the relationship will end or at least one person will be unhappy.

How do we choose to work things out when conflict arises? Unfortunately, many of us choose behaviors with a very strong feeling component, such as whining, crying, or complaining. We choose these behaviors because we believe that they will get us what we want, and often they seem to be effective, at least in the short run. Young children discover that tantrums usually aren't effective for long, so many learn to strike a mournful, pitiful pose, often accompanied by a painful series of sighs. Misery is a powerfully controlling behavior and many youngsters use it to get what they want. It is easy to say "no" to a screaming, kicking, angry child. It is much more difficult to say "no" to someone who looks so forlorn that you're afraid your refusal might utterly defeat them. Children whose manipulative, emotional behaviors get them what they want often grow into adults who use behaviors with powerful feeling components.

A friend of mine recently told me about a woman he knows who "suffers from depression. It's so bad she hasn't been able to work for a year." When I asked him if she was able to get out and enjoy herself at all, he told me, "Oh, sure. Last week we went to Fenway Park to see the Red Sox and she seemed O.K. to me. But people tell me she's got this depression and she can't work. It's too bad." People who are "too depressed to work" but quite capable of enjoying an evening out at the ball park have become masters at using misery behaviors in order to get what they want. This doesn't mean that their misery is artificial or that the pain they feel is not real. But until they develop other effective, satisfying behaviors, they will continue to ooze misery to retain some control over their lives.

Even though many people use behaviors with a strong feeling component to get what they want, this strategy is not productive if the goal is to have a good relationship. In a healthy relationship, both parties are able to satisfy their needs responsibly. Once someone tries to control you with their feelings, you will receive a strong negative signal because on some level you will know that you are being manipulated, which immediately prevents you from satisfying your need for freedom. Manipulation can come in positive forms (flattery) or negative forms (threats), but in either case, manipulative behavior can destroy a relationship.

Manipulative, controlling behaviors start to emerge very early in life. Young children often learn that a little extra misery can result in a second dessert or can change "no" into a reluctant "yes." How many times have you heard one child say to another, "If you don't let me go first, I'll never be your friend again"? Each of my children, at one time or another, has come up to me and said, "You're the best Dad in the whole world," and then immediately asked for something. Every time that has happened, the negative internal signal I received was jolting because I felt so manipulated. All of us can learn to eliminate some of our negative controlling behaviors, and as we do, our interpersonal relationships will improve.

In order to help children improve their relationships, there are specific behaviors you can model and teach them.

Teach children to tell others what they want in appropriate, unselfish ways

Like adults, children often believe that other people can read their minds and know what they want. This leads to a lot of needless misery. One objective of the activities in this book is to help children learn how to say what they really want, and improve their communication skills. For those of you who are afraid we will be creating a generation of self-centered youngsters, remember we are stressing that the children act responsibly. We are not encouraging selfishness, but we are fostering the development of communication skills which will allow children to meet their needs more effectively. We want to help children achieve reasonable, responsible wants, and not interfere with other people's attempts to satisfy their wants.

Compromise and Negotiate

These skills are probably the most important factors in maintaining any relationship over a long period of time. Since all long-term relationships will eventually involve conflict, the issue is not how to eliminate conflict, but how to handle it successfully. Like it or not, negotiation and compromise are the only methods we can use to resolve conflict responsibly. Other methods create winners and losers and are not conducive to a healthy relationship.

Negotiation and compromise are skills which allow both people in a conflict to get some of what they want and all of what they need. The alternative is that the more powerful person gets what he or she wants and the less powerful person becomes a loser. (Ironically, even the "winners" are frustrated because the process of winning can make it difficult to satisfy the need for love and

135

belonging.) Clearly, negotiation and compromise are preferable.

Children have difficulty understanding the terms "negotiation" and "compromise." However, I have found that my children are able to understand these terms when I say to them, "You'll have to find a fair way to work it out so that you're both happy." Then I step into the background and let them practice the arts of negotiation and compromise. Of course, since they are young, their efforts are sometimes less than satisfactory. Still, because I have a Quality World picture of being the father of adult children who are accomplished negotiators and compromisers, I encourage them to practice these skills in a safe environment and only intervene if one child is manipulating the other unmercifully. One morning as I worked on this book, Melanie and Greg were arguing—not an unusual occurrence. Melanie tried whining, hoping I would join forces with her so she could get what she wanted. After she had told me about her conflict with Greg, I asked, "What are you going to do now?" She just smiled and said, "I guess we'll have to work it out." It was a moment I'll treasure forever. Just as importantly, they did work it out, successfully and fairly.

Say "yes" as often as possible

You will be amazed at how many problems disappear! This is especially true when you are working with young children. When you say "yes," you are, by definition, a need-satisfying person and solidify your place in the Quality World of the child. On the other hand, when you say "no," you are telling someone that they can't have what they want. It's preferable, therefore, to say "yes" even if it has to be followed by a set of conditions. For example, saying "Yes, you can play with Billy once you have cleaned up your room" is preferable to saying "Absolutely not. Your room is a mess!"

Of course, there are times when adults need to say "no." Sometimes children want to do things that are against the rules or are dangerous. In such cases, it's both appropriate and responsible for the adult in charge to say "no." Children accept a "no" more readily from someone who is in their Quality World, someone who ordinarily helps them get what they want. But remember: if you do say "no," mean it. Don't weaken and change your mind.

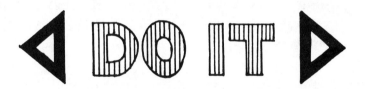

Learn To Say What You Want

Activity #1: Saying What You Want

In this activity, Do-It helps the children learn to communicate their wants in responsible ways and to plan effective behaviors to get what they want. The discussion should center on the following: (1) who the child needs to help him achieve what he wants; (2) what the child needs to say; and (3) when the child plans to say it. An important part of this activity is for children to learn how to communicate what they want in responsible, acceptable ways. The following example illustrates this process.

You: Hi, Do-It.

Do-It: Hi, everybody. I hope you have been making plans since I saw you last.

Y: Oh, yes, Do-It, we have. What have you got planned for today?

D: I wanted to do some more work on plans. Does someone want to help me? Any volunteers?

Y: I think Corey wants to volunteer.

D: Great. O.K., Corey. We're going to discuss something you want, who you need to tell, and how you're going to tell them, O.K.? What's something you want?

Corey: O.K., Do-It. That's easy. I want my father to take me to a basketball game.

D: Let's make a plan to solve that problem. First of all, does your father know that you want him to take you to a basketball game?

C: Well, he knows I like basketball, and he knows I had fun when we went to a game last year.

D: Sure, but have you told him recently that you'd like to go?

C: I guess not. I'll tell him tonight.

D: Not so fast, Corey. Let's figure out the best way to talk to your father.

C: The best way? Don't I just tell him to take me to the game?

D: You could. I'm not sure. Does your Dad work?

C: He's a carpenter.

D: Carpenters work pretty hard. Is he tired when he comes home from work?

C: You bet. He's exhausted and sometimes he's grumpy until after dinner.

D: Would it be fair to your Dad to ask him before dinner?

C: I get it. No, it wouldn't.

D: Corey, it's important for you to give your Dad some quiet time when he gets home. Let him know you understand that he has needs, too. He'll probably appreciate that.

C: So when should I ask him?

D: Well, what do you think?

C: He's usually in a pretty good mood after dinner. He sits around talking to my Mom and me. I could ask him then.

D: Sounds good. What exactly will you say?

C: Take me to a basketball game.

D: Do you think it might sound kind of selfish if you say it like that?

C: I don't mean it to be selfish. I had fun last time we went and I like doing stuff with my Dad. He's busy a lot, so I don't get a chance to do much with him.

D: That sounds different. Now it sounds like you want to go to the game so you can spend time with a person you care a lot about.

C: Well, that's what I want.

D: Then it's important to say that. That's what I mean when I say planning takes time and is a lot of hard work. You have to let your Dad know that you're not a selfish kid. You want to spend time with him.

C: I see what you mean.

D: When are you going to do it?

C: Well, tonight would be a good night, so I'll try to talk to him tonight.

D: Are you going to *try* to talk to him or are you *going* to talk to him?

C: I'm going to talk to him.

D: O.K., Corey. Good luck. Choose your words carefully, let your father know what you really mean, and I bet things will work out well.

C: Thanks, Do-It.

Y: Thanks, Do-It.

D: My pleasure. You know, I think all the kids would like to do what Corey just did.

Y: Well, guess what? We're all going to make plans, just like Corey did. Thanks for getting us started, Do-It. See you again soon.

Activity #2: A Happy Book Activity

Help children complete the "What I Want" page in *I'm Learning To Be Happy*. Be certain that the children pick wants which are responsible, appropriate, and achievable. Don't be afraid of making things too simple. Your goal is not to make sure children get everything they ever want. Your goal is to teach a *process* so children will have an effective model of how to communicate what they want to others.

What I Want

Something I really want.

_____

Someone who can help me get this.

_____

What I need to say to them so
they'll know what I want.

_____

When I plan to tell them what I
want. _____

We Can Work It Out

Activity #3: We Can Work It Out!

Use Do-It to introduce the "we can work it out" concepts of negotiation and compromise. It is probably best to discuss only one problem a day and do this activity for several days in a row. The best problems to use are those which have taken place in your class or in your home. "Real life" problems are always superior because they are relevant. Sometimes, however, it's easier to begin with a less threatening, artificial problem, so I have provided you with a few examples below. A dialogue with Do-It is included for the first problem as an illustration.

❶ The problem: Johnny and Nicolas are fighting over the last tractor to use in the sandbox.

You: What's up for today, Do-It?

Do-It: I'm going to tell you about two children who have a problem. I want to see if you kids can figure out a way for them to work it out so that both of them get what they need.

Y: Sounds like a good challenge. What's the problem?

D: Johnny and Nicolas are fighting over the last tractor in the sandbox. Both boys want it. What can they do so that they both get what they need, and there are no "losers"?

Y: Melanie, do you have a suggestion?

Melanie: Johnny could just let Nicolas use the tractor. Johnny probably gets whatever he wants anyway.

D: That's one possibility. Are there any problems with that solution? Greg?

Greg: Yeah. Johnny doesn't get to use the tractor so it's not fair.

D: Good point, Greg. So what can they do? Kristy?

Kristy: The boys could agree to take turns so that both get to use it some of the time.

D: Excellent! That's a great solution. That way both boys get what they need. They both win and nobody loses.

Y: Is that what you mean when you tell us that we have to learn to work it out?

D: That's right. Working it out means that everybody wins. If we want to get along with other people, we have to learn to work things out. Otherwise, we'll always have trouble with other people and that's not the way to be happy.

Y: Well, Do-It, we all want to thank you for everything you've taught us.

D: I've enjoyed myself. The important thing to remember is that we have to practice everything we've been talking about. But it's worth the work because in the end you'll learn how to make your life much happier.

Y: Thanks again, Do-It, and good-bye.

D: Good-bye, kids. Remember, I'll never be very far away. Whenever you want me, I'll be glad to help you find ways to lead happier lives. So long for now. Be happy!

❷ The Problem: Kristy and Jen have split a can of soda. Half of the soda is in the can and half is in a glass. Both girls want to drink from the can.

❸ The Problem: You allow the class to choose one movie from an appropriate list, to be shown at a special party. One half of the class wants to watch "Beauty and the Beast" and the other half wants to watch "Aladdin."

Activity #4: A Happy Book Activity

Children should not complete the "We Can Work It Out" page in *I'm Learning To Be Happy* until they have had some time to think about different ways people can solve problems. Once you feel they are ready to complete the individual exercise successfully, you can help them (1) identify a problem they had with someone else, and (2) what they did to work it out so that both people got what they needed. Make sure you help children choose situations where some negotiation and compromise actually took place. Don't choose situations where they used power to win or where they gave up everything to the other person just to avoid conflict. An important aspect of

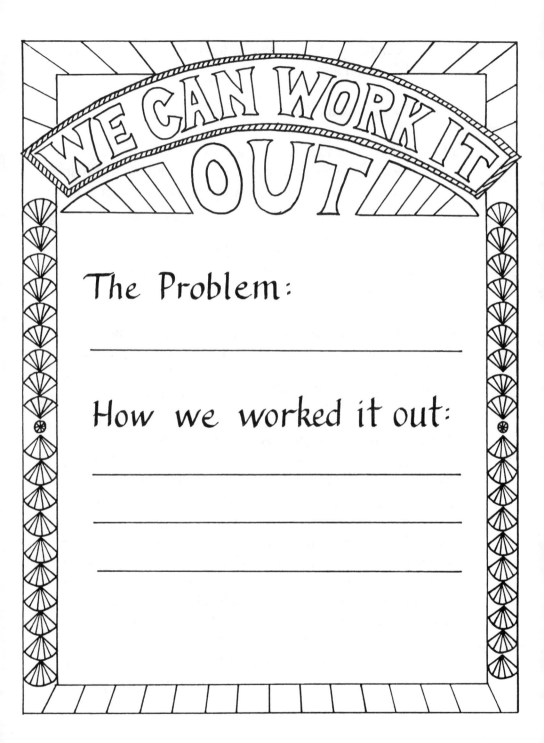

WE CAN WORK IT OUT

The Problem:

_____

How we worked it out:

_____

_____

_____

this activity is that children realize they have worked things out successfully. As with many of the other activities they have done, a successful experience helps to build their self-esteem.

Make Someone's Day

Activity #5: Positive Bombardment!

Here is a delightful activity whose objective is to have children practice saying positive things about other people. This activity is wonderful for group time at schools or at dinner with families. Have every person in the group say one positive thing about each other person. (At the dinner table, everyone should participate in this activity, regardless of their age!) This will give children practice in complimenting other people and help them build positive relationships. Also, hearing good things about themselves helps to satisfy their needs for love and power. This activity is almost always a wonderful success. It can make meal time a more positive experience in any home. I strongly urge everyone to make this activity a regular part of your routine, not a one- or two-time event.

Activity #6: A Happy Book Activity

Have individual children complete the "It's Nice To Be Nice" page in *I'm Learning To Be Happy* where they are asked to indicate something positive they have said to three other people during the past week. It is best to do this soon after the "Positive Bombardment" so that children will not have difficulty thinking of the nice things they have been saying recently.

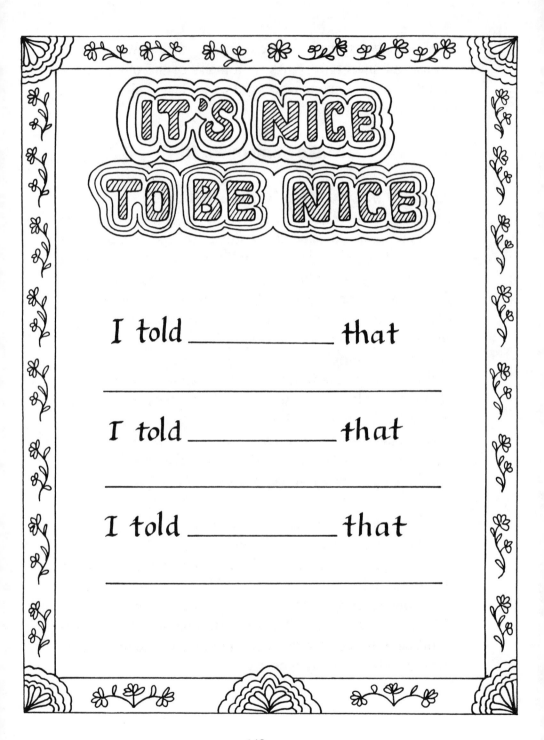

IT'S NICE TO BE NICE

I told _____ that

_____

I told _____ that

_____

I told _____ that

_____

Chapter Eight: Creativity

Creativity is part of our genetic structure. Our brains are constantly generating new behaviors which we could select in our efforts to solve problems and meet our needs more effectively. Even those of us who claim not to be particularly creative have a creative system which is always "on." The problem is that our creativity isn't programmed to evaluate—to determine if an idea is good or bad, responsible or irresponsible, practical or impractical. It simply creates, whether we want it to or not. As thinking human beings, however, we are able to evaluate the many behavioral possibilities our creative systems develop.

Young children can be taught to be more creative in two ways. First, you can teach them the process of brainstorming. If you have conducted the activities suggested in this book, then your children have already been exposed to this process. I recommend brainstorming as a regular problem-solving technique to use with children. It teaches them that alternatives are always available to choose from. It helps children appreciate that problems frequently have multiple solutions, and consequently, it helps prevent children from falling into the "right or wrong" answer trap. Brainstorming is a fun activity which encourages children to focus upon the thinking component of behavior, expanding their cognitive abilities. Finally, brainstorming fosters creativity.

A second avenue to creativity, a "quiet time" activity, is something that can be integrated into an educational program or may be done with children at home. Just as adults can gain access to their creativity by regularly engaging in a non-competitive, relaxing, and solitary activity, children can start to establish similar behavioral patterns in their lives. In our effort to provide "meaningful" and "structured" experiences for our children, many of us have overscheduled our children's days. While structure is a wonderful thing, children whose lives are overly structured have less ability to utilize unstructured time responsibly and effectively. Such children tend to be less discriminating in their use of creative behaviors. Because their overly structured lives dictate to them how they should behave at all times. They become "bored" when there is nothing on the agenda.

All children can profit from 20-30 minutes each day of "quiet time." This time should not be spent watching TV or socializing. Children should spend this time entertaining themselves, developing their creative systems. Building with blocks, playing a musical instrument, looking at books, coloring, drawing, painting, working with clay, or "just thinking" are all appropriate behaviors during quiet time. All activities should have the following characteristics:

(1) They should be non-competitive.

(2) They should not require a great deal of effort and the child should be able to do them reasonably well.

(3) The child should be able to do them alone.

(4) Most importantly, the child should be completely self-accepting during this time. If the child is at all self-critical when doing the activities, much of the therapeutic and creative value will be lost.

Adults also profit from a daily "quiet time." We live in a stressful society and have paid a high price, including denying ourselves access to the positive creative solutions our behavioral system has to offer. Even those of you who will never incorporate such a routine into your daily lives because "I just don't have the time," probably can appreciate its value. If that's the case, teach your children from the earliest possible age to slow down each day, to take time for themselves, to have a time every day when they are completely self-accepting, listening to their creative selves. Behaviors that become habits are difficult to change. Why not turn that sometimes frustrating fact into an advantage by helping children develop behavioral habits which will strengthen them? (For more information about how to tap into your own creative system, read *Positive Addiction* by Dr. William Glasser.)

Don't expect that children will become noticeably more creative after a daily "quiet time" routine has been established at home or in school. Young children tend to be more creative than adults anyway. They need to create new behaviors regularly because they have fewer organized behaviors in their repertoires. In addition, they have fewer barriers and inhibitions to overcome. What you offer children will not necessarily enhance their creativity immediately, but it will provide them with a model for behavior which will become increasingly valuable to them as they get older. The immediate benefit to children is that they will be engaging in a self-accepting activity which they enjoy every day. That, by itself, will help build strength and lead to greater happiness.

Activity #1: Quiet Time

Set aside a half-hour, or whatever time you can manage, for children to do individual "quiet time" activities. Discuss with the children the characteristics of an appropriate quiet-time activity, then give the children some time to make suggestions. Each child should pick an activity for the quiet time and do it. Daydreaming, thinking, doodling, and even "nothing" are all acceptable activities.

Summary

As Part II draws to a close, it's important to summarize what we can do to help young children.

We can teach them about the basic needs which will motivate them for the rest of their lives.

We can teach them about the specific Quality World pictures they develop to satisfy these basic needs.

We can teach them to recognize both their positive and negative signals.

We can teach them that they choose how to act, even if they don't have direct control over how they feel.

We can teach them that all behaviors have consequences and that they create most of their pleasure and their pain.

We can teach them how to develop options so that they have a better chance of getting what they need in a responsible way.

We can teach them how to plan, to organize a series of behaviors, so they can responsibly get more of what they want.

We can teach them to be responsible, to behave in ways that allow other children to satisfy their needs.

We can teach them how to have better access to their creative selves.

In short, we can
TEACH THEM TO BE HAPPY!

Activities for
a Balanced Classroom

In *Teach Them To Be Happy* I have given suggestions about how to work with children at school and at home to help them experience happiness by learning to satisfy their basic needs regularly and in a balanced way. Teachers would benefit enormously if they had a pool of activities to choose from which would ensure that all children have an opportunity to satisfy their needs for love, power, fun, and freedom every day.

I invite you to participate in a project, the creation of a book filled with age-appropriate, satisfying Activities for a Balanced Classroom. Educators will be able to select from model activities which their colleagues have found to be successful in such a way as to achieve even greater balance in their programs.

If you are interested in contributing one (or several) of your favorite, successful activities, I would be delighted to hear from you. Simply supply the information listed below with as much detail as possible. Feel free to ask your colleagues if they would be interested in participating.

Contributors are encouraged to send activities as soon as possible. Publication will commence once a sufficient number of quality contributions have been received. Contributors whose activities are selected for publication will be acknowledged as contributors and will be given a complimentary copy of the the first edition of the book in which their contribution appears. Accepted contributions may be edited and their final form may differ somewhat from what is provided.

Submission Form for
Activities for a Balanced Classroom

All contributions should be typed, double spaced, and include all of the information requested below. Address all correspondence to: Robert A. Sullo, PO Box 1336, Sandwich, MA 02563.

① Name of Activity:

② Indicate the need or needs addressed by this activity:
LOVE   POWER   FUN   FREEDOM

③ Level for which this activity is most appropriate (please indicate only one):   pre-school
                                                                                                         grades K-1
                                                                                                         grades 2-3

④ Content Area:
language arts	math	health & safety
social studies	art	drama
science	music	other (please specify)

⑤ Objective of the activity: (Exactly what are the children expected to get from this activity?)

⑥ Materials required:

⑦ Procedure: (Be as specific as possible, explaining exactly how to do this activity.)

⑧ Any additional comments that you think might be helpful: (i.e., Is the activity easy or difficult to organize? Is the activity one which can be done at any time, or should the group be together for a while before it is attempted? etc.)

⑨ Contributor's name as you wish it to appear:

⑩ Your personal address and telephone number: (This information is for my use only, in case I need to contact you to get information, seek clarification, etc. Only your city or town and state will be published.)

In accordance with the Copyright Revision Act of 1976, you must submit the following statement, signed, before your submission can be considered for publication:

"In consideration of Robert A. Sullo taking action in reviewing and editing my submission, the author(s) undersigned hereby transfer, assign, or otherwise convey all copyright ownership to Robert A. Sullo in the event such work is published by him."

Contributor's Signature and Date:

Suggestions for Further Reading

Books about Control Theory and Reality Therapy

Glasser, William. *Reality Therapy*. New York: HarperCollins, 1969. This pioneer book provides a fascinating account of the use of Reality Therapy with difficult cases.

Glasser, William. *Positive Addiction.* New York: HarperCollins, 1976. A guide to add positively addicting, strength-building activities to your life.

Glasser, William. *Control Theory*. New York: HarperCollins, 1984. A complete description of the theory upon which the process of Reality Therapy is built.

Glasser, William. *Control Theory in the Classroom.* New York: HarperCollins, 1986. Details how to implement Control Theory principles in school systems. Emphasis on issues in secondary schools.

Glasser, William. *The Quality School: Managing Students Without Coercion*. New York: HarperCollins, 1990. Provides suggestions based on lead management to help all students do quality work.

Glasser, William. *The Quality School Teacher*. New York: HarperCollins, 1993. Offers teachers specific suggestions for implementing Quality School concepts in their classrooms.

Good, E. Perry. *In Pursuit of Happiness*. Chapel Hill, NC: New View, 1987. Details the essential elements of Control Theory and provides useful activities designed to help people take more effective control of their lives.

Good, E. Perry. *Helping Kids Help Themselves*. Chapel Hill, NC: New View, 1992. Although we cannot force kids to be responsible and independent, we can help them move in this direction by teaching them to self-evaluate what they are doing.

Books about Child Development

Brazelton, T. Berry. *Toddlers and Parents*. New York: Delacourte Press, 1974. A pediatrician from Children's Hospital in Boston describes the characteristics of very young children and the stresses of child-rearing.

Elkind, David. *Miseducation: Preschoolers at Risk*. Massachusetts: Addison-Wesley, 1987. A plea to parents to let children develop naturally without the introduction of formal instruction at too young an age. Recommended for parents of preschoolers.

Elkind, David. *The Hurried Child*. Massachusetts: Addison-Wesley, 1981. An examination of the consequences of hurrying child growth, and suggestions for a less stressful method of raising children. Emphasis on children in elementary school.

Elkind, David. *All Grown Up and No Place To Go*. Massachusetts: Addison-Wesley, 1984. Concentrates on the developmental tasks and challenges of adolescence, including the need to develop an independent identity.

Gossen, Diane. *My Child is a Pleasure to Live With*. Saskatchewan, Canada: Chelsom Consultants, 1988. Provides exercises for evaluating parenting skills and improving parent-child relationships.

Likona, Thomas. *Raising Good Children*. New York: Bantam, 1983. For parents interested in the moral development of children. Builds upon the pioneer work on moral reasoning of Lawrence Kohlberg.

Smith, Glenn and Kathy Tomberlin. *Quality Times for Quality Kids*. North Carolina: New View Publications, 1992. Provides helpful ideas for conducting group activities and helping children build self-esteem.

White, Burton. *Educating the Infant and Toddler*. Massachusetts Lexington Books, 1988. Details the stages of development with an emphasis in how early experiences lay the foundation for all social and intellectual development.

About the Author

Bob Sullo has been a public educator for nearly twenty years, having taught English for eight years before becoming a counselor and school psychologist. During this time, Bob has worked with students from pre-kindergarten through high school. He conducts numerous workshops for both parents and teachers based on the principles of Reality Therapy.

After receiving a Master of Arts in Teaching degree, Bob earned a Certificate of Advanced Educational Specialization in School Psychology from Boston College. He is a faculty member of the Institute for Reality Therapy and is a nationally certified school psychologist.

Bob and his wife Laurie live on Cape Cod in Sandwich, Massachusetts, with their children Kristy, Greg, and Melanie.

Author Speaking Engagements

For information regarding speaking engagements by Robert A. Sullo, contact the author at P. O. Box 1336, Sandwich, MA 02563 or phone (508) 888-7627.